The

BLACK
BELT
Memory
Jogger™

**A Desktop Guide for
Six Sigma Success**

Six Sigma Academy

**First Edition
GOAL/QPC**

The Black Belt Memory Jogger™

Desktop Guide
© 2002 by GOAL/QPC and Six Sigma Academy.
All rights reserved.

Six Sigma is a federally registered trademark of Motorola, Inc.
MINITAB is a trademark of Minitab, Inc.

Six Sigma Academy

Therese Costich-Sicker, *Project Manager*
Paul Sheehy, *Writer*
Philip Samuel, Ph.D., *Copy Editor*
Daniel Navarro, *Writer*
Terry Ziemer, Ph.D., *Copy Editor*
Robert Silvers, *Writer*
Victoria Keyes, *Writer*
Shannon Godden, *Copy Editor*
John Dziark, *Copy Editor*
Tylar Burton, *Copy Editor*
Marcia Lemmons, *Copy Editor*
Deb Dixon, *Writer*

GOAL/QPC

Daniel Picard, *Editor*
Danielle Page, *Production*
Michele Kierstead, *Cover Design, Graphics, and Layout*
Bob Page, *Project Manager*

GOAL/QPC

12B Manor Parkway, Salem, NH 03079-2862
Toll free: 800-643-4316 **or** 603-890-8800
Fax: 603-870-9122
E-mail: service@goalqpc.com
Web site: www.goalqpc.com

Printed in the United States of America
First Edition   10 9 8 7 6 5 4 3 2 1
ISBN 1-57681-054-2

Acknowledgments

Our sincerest thanks to the people and organizations who contributed suggestions and encouragement or who gave us permission to adapt their charts, tables, and other information.

We are especially grateful to a long-time friend and supporter of GOAL/QPC, Larry Smith of Ford Motor Company, who provided the inspiration for this book.

We are indebted to the following reviewers who ensured that the finished book aligned with expectations:

Lyn Dolson Pugh, Katherine Calvert, Michael G. Thibeau, *Dow Chemical Company*; Larry R. Smith, *Ford Motor Company*; Marc Richardson, *JAE Oregon, Inc.*; Kristi Brown, *Wal-Mart*; David M. Oberholtzer, *Raytheon Company*; Richard K. Bergeron, *Seagate Inc.*

We are also grateful for those who shared with us their vision for this book:

Raj Gohil, *AT&T Corporate Quality*; Rip Stauffer, *BlueFire Partners*; Jeff Karl, *Bombadier Regional Aircraft*; C. Gregory Brown, *Citigroup*; Randy Fach, *Dove Consulting*; Kui-Sun Yim, *Ford Motor Company*; Cheryl Rienzo, *Honeywell, Inc.*; David Fogelson, *Honeywell, Inc.*; Eric Jakubowski, *Motorola, Inc.*; John Thomasson, *NCR Corporation*; Russell Soukup, *Pemstar, Inc.*; Bill Fechter, Ph.D., *Productivity Inc.*; Jay P. Patel, *Quality & Productivity Solutions, Inc.*; Allen C. Rothman, *Quad Tech, Inc.*; Lynda Owens, Neal Mackertich, *Raytheon Company*; Swaminathan Balachandran, *University of Wisconsin–Platteville.*

Foreword

Six Sigma programs have made tremendous contributions to many organizations worldwide, and we at GOAL/QPC anticipate that the long-term benefits will accrue as more organizations learn and apply Six Sigma.

However, as Six Sigma becomes more commonplace, it will be accompanied by increased pressure to quickly train Black Belts and to produce results. For some prospective Black Belts, the learning challenge will be daunting and the post-training performance expectations even more so.

To help support new and current Black Belts, we decided to create a Memory Jogger specifically for their needs. We partnered with Six Sigma Academy and melded their extensive knowledge and experience in Six Sigma tools and methods with GOAL/QPC's skill in producing Memory Jogger™ pocket guides. In preparing this guide, we are assuming that users are familiar with DMAIC processes, the basics of quality management, and the basic quality tools found in *The Memory Jogger™ II*.

The Black Belt Memory Jogger™ serves double duty as a training document for new Black Belts and a ready reference to support their real-world performance.

With the help of many reviewers, the experts and practitioners who worked on this project have assembled the necessary information to support successful Black Belt performance. We trust you will agree.

Bob Page
GOAL/QPC

Table of Contents

 **Introduction**

What is Six Sigma?

The Six Sigma methodologies are a business philosophy and initiative that enables world-class quality and continuous improvement to achieve the highest level of customer satisfaction. Metrics are established that align an organization's strategic goals and values to that of their customer's needs and expectations.

Sigma (σ) represents a unit of measurement that designates the distribution or spread about the mean (average) of a process. In business, a sigma value is a metric that represents how well a process is performing and how often a defect is likely to occur. The higher the sigma value, the less variation and fewer defects the process will have. Six Sigma is the new standard of excellence at only 3.4 defects per million opportunities (DPMO).

How does it work?

The Six Sigma philosophy uses data and statistical tools to systematically improve processes and sustain process improvements. Process metrics are evaluated based on a comparison of average and variation to performance specifications or targets.

The methodology is a project-focused approach consisting of five phases: Define, Measure, Analyze, Improve, and Control. Projects are selected and *Defined* from business, operational, and customer needs, based on their linkage to executive strategies. In the *Measure* phase, tools are applied to validate the measurement system and to characterize the process. In the *Analyze* and *Improve* phases, sources of variation are identified, a statistical relationship between the process input and output variables is established, and the process performance is optimized. The *Control* phase applies traditional and statistical tools to sustain process improvements. Emphasis is placed on controlling the key process inputs to consistently achieve key process outputs.

The DMAIC Model

What is it?

The DMAIC model is a set of tools outlined in five phases that are used to characterize and optimize both business and industrial processes. Each project must complete the five phases in chronological order.

Define Phase

In the Define phase, the customer needs are stated and the processes and products to be improved are identified.

Steps	Activities/Tools	Output(s)
Create problem statement	• Define process to improve • Define project objectives • Identify project stakeholders • Identify customers	• Problem statement • Project scope • Project goals
Identify CTQs	• CT Trees	• Identified customer needs
Define performance standards	• Identify performance measures • Financial analysis • High-level process mapping	• Gap analysis • Business impact (project savings) • Project definition • Project charter • Project plan/ timeline • High-level process map • Definition of performance measures

Measure Phase

The Measure phase determines the baseline and target performance of the process, defines the input/output variables of the process, and validates the measurement systems.

Steps	Activities/Tools	Output(s)
Understand process and validate measurement system	• Process-map the as-is process • Identify process inputs/outputs • Collect data • Evaluate measurement system of process y's	• Detailed process map • Identified process output variables (POV) – (y's) and their measurements • Identified process input variables (PIV) – (x's) • Validated performance data • Measurement system capability on y's • Data collection/sampling plan
Determine process capability	• Control charts on process y's • Capability analysis • Graphical techniques	• Baseline control charts • Baseline capability • DPMO • Z value
Finalize performance objectives	• Cause and effect analysis • Create FMEA • Review of project goals and plan	• Revised project goals • Quantified project objectives • Validated financial goals • Revised project plan • Cause and effect relationships • Prioritized risk

Analyze Phase

The Analyze phase uses data to establish the key process inputs that affect the process outputs.

Steps	Activities/Tools	Output(s)
Identify sources of variation	• Detailed process map • Brainstorming • Fishbone diagram • Cause & Effect Matrix • FMEA • SPC on x's and y's • MSA on x's	• Identified sources of variation • Identified potential leverage variables (KPIVs) • Updated process map • Updated FMEA
Screen potential causes	• Graphical analysis • Hypothesis testing • Multi-Vari analysis • Correlation and regression analysis	• Potential x's critical to process performance • Identified improvement opportunities • Data on KPIVs • Statistical analysis of data

Improve Phase

The Improve phase identifies the improvements to optimize the outputs and eliminate / reduce defects and variation. It identifies x's and determines the $y = f(x)$ relationship, and statistically validates the new process operating conditions.

Steps	Activities/Tools	Output(s)
Determine variable relationship $y = f(x)$	• Designed experiments • Regression analysis • ANOVA • Simulation	• Relationships between x's and y's • KPIV settings for optimum process outputs and minimum output variation
Establish operating tolerances	• Establish relationships between x's and y's • Use optimum settings for x's • Determine new process capability • Cost/benefit analysis	• Optimum robust settings for x's with tolerances • Updated project plan • Established implementation plan
Confirm results and validate improvements	• Confirmation experiments • Process maps • MSA • Control charts • Process capability • Corrective actions	• Updated process maps, FMEA, data collection • Pilot run • Validated measurement systems after improvements (x's and y's) • Improved capability

Control Phase

The Control phase documents, monitors, and assigns accountability for sustaining the gains made by the process improvements.

Steps	Activities/Tools	Output(s)
Redefine process capabilities x's and y's	• Control plan SPC on x's and y's • Capability analysis	• Control plan • Control charts • DPMO • Z
Implement process control	• Mistake proofing • Standard procedures • Accountability audits • Responsibility audits • Finalize transition to process owner • FMEA • Preventive maintenance • Gauge control plans	• Validated control process • Sustained performance • Monitoring plan • Recalculated FMEA RPN • System changes to institutionalize improvement
Complete project documentation	• Financial validation • Team meeting with stakeholders and customer • Project tracking completion • Identify replication of project results opportunities	• Lessons learned/ best practices • Communicated project success • Project report • Executive summary • Final deliverables • Customer feedback

©2002 GOAL/QPC,
Six Sigma Academy

 **Roles and Responsibilities**

Why is understanding roles and responsibilities important?

Prior to deployment, during deployment, and in transition to the organization, there are critical roles and responsibilities that ensure Six Sigma methodologies become ingrained in the business. Understanding who is responsible for each activity will allow for an effective deployment.

Executives

- Create the vision for the Six Sigma initiative.
- Define the strategic goals and measures of the organization.
- Establish the business targets.
- Create an environment within the organization that will promote the use of the Six Sigma methodology and tools.

Senior Deployment Champion

- Is responsible for the day-to-day management of Six Sigma throughout the entire organization.
- Designs the Six Sigma infrastructure and support systems (training, project approvals, human resources, reporting systems, etc.)
- Uses performance goals to get business unit leaders on board.
- Reports to and updates the executives on the progress of deployment.
- Acts as a liaison between the executives and deployment champions.
- Works with deployment champions to develop a communication plan for the organization.

Deployment Champion

- Is responsible for the deployment of Six Sigma within his/her division or business unit.
- Works with the leaders of the division or business unit to determine their goals and objectives and ensure that they are aligned with the executives.
- Conducts a Critical To flowdown to identify areas of opportunities that are aligned with the business goals.
- Facilitates the identification and prioritization of projects.
- Establishes and executes training plans.
- Develops a communication plan for the division or business unit.
- Reports the deployment status of the division or business unit to the senior deployment champion.
- Selects the project champions.
- Removes barriers for the team.

Project Champion

- Selects and mentors Black Belts.
- Leads in project identification, prioritization, and defining the project scope.
- Removes barriers for Black Belts and aligns resources.
- Works with deployment champions to implement the Six Sigma infrastructure.
- Communicates progress of Six Sigma projects to the deployment champion and process owners.

Master Black Belt

- Is an expert on Six Sigma tools and concepts.
- Trains Black Belts and ensures they are properly applying the methodology and tools.
- Coaches and mentors Black Belts and Green Belts.

- Maintains the training material and updates it if necessary.
- Works high-level projects, many of which are across divisions or business units.
- Assists champions and process owners with project selection, project management, and Six Sigma administration.

Black Belt

- Is responsible for leading, executing, and completing DMAIC projects.
- Teaches team members the Six Sigma methodology and tools.
- Assists in identifying project opportunities and refining project details and scope.
- Reports progress to the project champions and the process owners.
- Transfers knowledge to other Black Belts and the organization.
- Mentors Green Belts.

Process Owner

- Is a team member.
- Takes ownership of the project when it is complete.
- Is responsible for maintaining the project's gains.
- Removes barriers for Black Belts.

Green Belt

- Is trained in a subset of the Six Sigma methodology and tools.
- Works small scope projects, typically in his/her respective work area.
- Can be an effective team member on a Black Belt team.

Finance Champion

- Estimates and certifies project savings.
- Establishes clear criteria on hard and soft savings.
- Works with deployment champions to identify potential project opportunities.
- Assigns a finance representative to each Black Belt team.

Information Technology Champion

- Ensures computer and software resourcing.
- Works with Black Belt teams to access data from existing databases.
- Works with Black Belt teams to develop an electronic project tracking system to collect, store, analyze, and report project data.
- Provides training on the project tracking system.
- Develops a reporting system to keep executives and project champions informed about progress in meeting goals and targets.

Human Resources Champion

- Identifies roles and responsibilities for Master Black Belts, Black Belts, and Green Belts.
- Works with the project champions to develop a Master Black Belt, Black Belt, and Green Belt selection process.
- Develops a career path transition process for Master Black Belts and Black Belts.
- Works with the senior deployment champion and project champions to determine rewards and recognition for Master Black Belts, Black Belts, Green Belts, and teams.

Project Management

(**Note:** An in-depth discussion of the components of project management is beyond the scope of this book. For a complete description, please refer to the *Project Management Memory Jogger™*.)

Why use it?

Project management:

- Defines expected timelines and the project scope.
- Focuses time and resources to meet the customer requirements for a project.
- Reduces duplication of effort.
- Identifies problem areas and risk.
- Serves as a communication tool.

What does it do?

It assigns roles, responsibilities, and timing of deliverables to allow each person to know what his or her tasks are and when they are due. It also provides the project manager with a way to monitor progress in order to take action when appropriate.

How do I do it?

There are four basic phases in project management: 1) Creating a project charter, 2) Creating a project plan, 3) Executing and monitoring the plan, and 4) Completing (closing out) the project.

Project Charter

Why do it?

A project charter defines the customer needs, project scope, project goals, project success criteria, team members, and project deadlines.

How do I do it?

1. Create a problem statement that describes the project.

2. Identify the customer needs.

3. Identify the project goals, project success criteria, and final deliverable for the project.

4. Identify the roles and responsibilities of team members.

5. Identify the stakeholders and resource owners for project approval.

Project Plan

Why do it?

The project plan identifies all the work to be done, who will do the work, and when the work will get done.

How do I do it?

1. Identify the work to be done.

   - Use a work breakdown structure (WBS) to identify the work to be done. The WBS is a hierarchical grouping of project tasks that organizes and defines the total project work.

A Work Breakdown Structure
for the Development of
an Educational Course

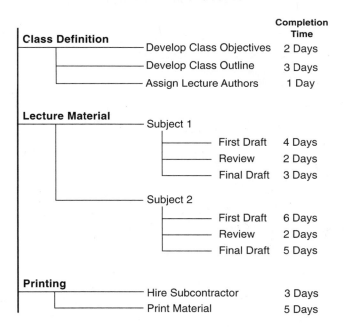

		Completion Time
Class Definition	Develop Class Objectives	2 Days
	Develop Class Outline	3 Days
	Assign Lecture Authors	1 Day
Lecture Material	Subject 1	
	First Draft	4 Days
	Review	2 Days
	Final Draft	3 Days
	Subject 2	
	First Draft	6 Days
	Review	2 Days
	Final Draft	5 Days
Printing	Hire Subcontractor	3 Days
	Print Material	5 Days

2. Assign resources and estimate the time duration.

- For each task identified in the WBS, resources must be assigned and a time duration estimated. To document these activities, use an accountability matrix. The accountability matrix documents who is accountable for a particular task, who's input is required to complete a task, who is required to review the task, and who is required to sign-off on the task completion.

An Accountability Matrix for the Educational Course WBS

ID	Task	Duration (Days)	Tim	Alex	Julia
1	Class Definition			A	
1.1	Develop Class Objectives	2	A	R	I
1.2	Develop Class Outline	3	A	R	I
1.3	Assign Lecture Authors	1		A	
2	Lecture Material			A	
2.1	Subject 1		A		
2.1.1	First Draft	4	A		I
2.1.2	Review	2	A	R	
2.1.3	Final Draft	3	A	S	I
2.2	Subject 2				A
2.2.1	First Draft	6	I		A
2.2.2	Review	2		R	A
2.2.3	Final Draft	5	I	S	A
3	Printing			A	
3.1	Hire Subcontractor	3		A	
3.2	Print Material	5	I	A	I

Key	
A	Accountable
R	Review Required
I	Input Required
S	Sign-off Required

©2002 GOAL/QPC, Six Sigma Academy

3. **Develop a project schedule.**

 • Identify the critical path of the project on an Activity Network Diagram. The critical path is the shortest possible time to complete the project from the first task to the last task.

An Activity Network Diagram
for the Educational Course Development

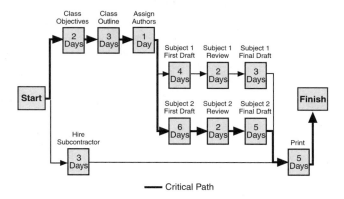

—— Critical Path

 • Draw a Gantt Chart displaying the project tasks and their duration. Add appropriate milestones in the Gantt Chart.

Team-Defined Milestones and Gantt Chart from the Educational Course Activity Network Diagram

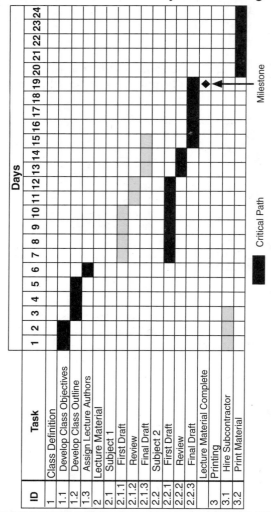

Days

ID	Task	1	2	3	4	5	6	7	8	9	10	11	12	13	14	15	16	17	18	19	20	21	22	23	24
1	Class Definition																								
1.1	Develop Class Objectives																								
1.2	Develop Class Outline																								
1.3	Assign Lecture Authors																								
2	Lecture Material																								
2.1	Subject 1																								
2.1.1	First Draft																								
2.1.2	Review																								
2.1.3	Final Draft																								
2.2	Subject 2																								
2.2.1	First Draft																								
2.2.2	Review																								
2.2.3	Final Draft																								
	Lecture Material Complete																								
3	Printing																								
3.1	Hire Subcontractor																								
3.2	Print Material																								

◆ Milestone

■ Critical Path

Project Execution and Monitoring

Why do it?

Once the project plan has been completed, it is time to execute the project and monitor its progress. It is important to monitor the project to ensure timely deliverables that stay within budget.

How do I do it?

Executing the project is doing the tasks assigned. Monitoring the project is done by holding regular team meetings to update the progress of the activities. At these meetings, the people accountable for each task should give a "percent complete" status of their particular task. Any gaps or risks in completing the program should be identified at this time and recovery plans put in place. An action item list for the project should be developed and the schedule should be updated to show any delays in task completion or milestone dates.

Project Close Out

Why do it?

Formally closing out the project ensures that future teams will benefit from the documented lessons learned so that they can duplicate successes and avoid problems the team encountered.

How do I do it?

1. **Hold a team meeting with the customers and stakeholders of the project to solicit feedback on opportunities for improvement and to identify things that were done well.**

2. Develop and document lessons learned.

- The team should review the results from the team meeting and its own personal experience, and document the lessons learned.

3. Create a project report.

- The team should create a report that summarizes the team's activities on the project. The report should include all the information from the project charter, an executive summary on the project, the lessons learned on the project, a description of the final deliverable, and the customers' feedback. The report should be archived and a copy should be made available to all those involved and affected by the project.

 **Critical To Flowdown**

Why use it?

During the Define phase, project champions and Black Belts use Critical To Trees (CT Trees) and Critical To Matrices (CT Matrices) as tools to define DMAIC projects. The CT Tree is used as a method to analyze customer requirement flowdown to ensure that what the organization is working on is critical to its business and its customers and strikes a balance between both. The CT Matrix identifies customer requirements and links these requirements in a matrix fashion to those organizational processes most likely to impact them. (Both of these tools consider customers to be either the external or internal users of the product or service.)

What does it do?

The CT Tree is a tool that translates needs considered vital by the customer into product and service characteristics, and links these characteristics to organizational processes. The CT Matrix is a simplified version of a Quality Function Deployment (QFD). A single Black Belt project could employ CT Trees and CT Matrices at various levels within a process.

Before creating a CT Tree or CT Matrix, certain terms to describe characteristics in these tools must be defined:

- *Critical To Satisfaction* (CTS) characteristics relate specifically to the satisfaction of the customer. The customer will typically define satisfaction in one of three ways:

   1. *Critical To Quality* (CTQ) characteristics are product, service, and/or transactional characteristics that significantly influence one or more CTSs in terms of quality.

2. *Critical To Delivery* (CTD) characteristics are product, service, and/or transactional characteristics that significantly influence one or more CTSs in terms of delivery (or cycle).

3. *Critical To Cost* (CTC) characteristics are product, service, and/or transactional characteristics that significantly influence one or more CTSs in terms of cost.

• *Critical to the Process* (CTP) characteristics are process parameters that significantly influence a CTQ, CTD, and/or CTC.

For the equation $y = f(x_1, x_2, ... x_n)$, the CTQ, CTD, or CTC characteristics represent the dependent variable (y), and the CTP characteristics represent the independent variables (x's).

The CTQ, CTD, and CTC are "opportunities for nonconformance" that must be measured and reported, while the CTP represents "control opportunities."

How do I do it?

There are two types of trees or flowdowns that need to be created to strike a balance between the business and the customer: *process trees* and *product trees*.

• A *process tree* is a breakdown of the organization's engineering, manufacturing, service, and transaction processes. CTPs are identified at the lowest level of this tree.

• A *product tree* is a hierarchical breakdown of the organization's product or service, which allows a visualization of the CTQ, CTD, and CTC characteristics at each level of the hierarchy.

A typical CTX product tree is shown in the following figure. The numbers in the text that follows correspond to the numbers in circles in the graphic.

A CTX Product Tree or Flowdown

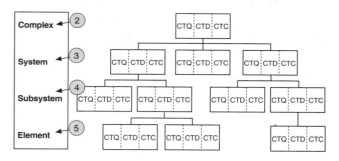

1. Critical requirements for quality, delivery, and cost are translated from the CTS characteristics.

2. The complex level is the first level of the product tree and describes the final product or service that is delivered to the customer. CTQs, CTDs, and CTCs can be found at this level and are usually expressed as a function of the immediate lower level characteristics: CTQ-complex $= f$ (CTQ-system$_1$, ... CTQ-system$_n$).

3. The system level is a more detailed breakdown of the complex level. CTQs, CTDs, and CTCs can be found at this level and are usually expressed as a function of the immediate lower level characteristics: CTQ-system $= f$ (CTQ-subsystem$_1$, ... CTQ-subsystem$_n$).

4. The subsystem level is a more detailed breakdown of the system level. CTQs, CTDs, and CTCs can be found at this level and are usually expressed as a function of the

immediate lower level characteristics: CTQ-system = f (CTQ-element$_1$, ... CTQ-element$_n$).

5. The element level is the lowest level of the tree. Its components are not divisible. CTQs, CTDs, and CTCs can be found at this level.

The size of the tree is dependent on the complexity of the product or service (e.g., a spark plug is less complex than a car and would therefore have a less complex CT Tree). Described in the following figure is a tree that looks at the product a business might sell to a customer.

Product Flowdown

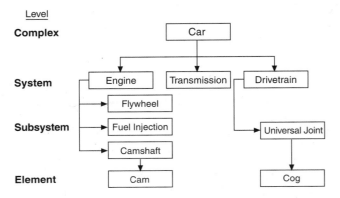

A given product or service at any level of the hierarchy in this tree can have quality, delivery, and/or cost issues that concern customers. Within the hierarchy, the organization must consider whether it is satisfying those customer needs.

A CTX process tree for the major processes that support the engineering, manufacturing, marketing, and sales of this car can also be created, as described in the figure on the next page.

Process Flowdown

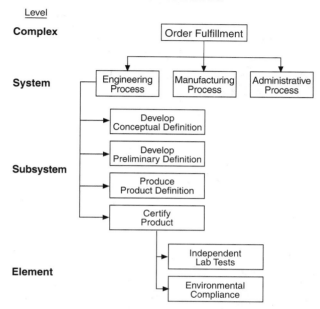

Level

Complex

Order Fulfillment

System

Engineering Process · Manufacturing Process · Administrative Process

Subsystem

Develop Conceptual Definition

Develop Preliminary Definition

Produce Product Definition

Certify Product

Element

Independent Lab Tests

Environmental Compliance

This process tree will help identify the individual x's that can potentially impact the individual y's of a product.

To determine which product and/or process needs the most attention the organization will create a CT Matrix. The CT Matrix, like the CT Tree, is developed by the project champion and the Black Belt, together with a team that collectively has process/product knowledge and, to the greatest extent possible, an understanding of the voice of the customer. It is owned by the product or process owner.

Once the product tree has been developed and customer requirements (CTS) identified, the organization can use a CT Matrix to determine which processes are most likely to impact those CTS requirements, as shown in the figure on the next page.

A CT Matrix

Process Tree / Subsystem Level \ Product Tree / Complex Level	Needs to achieve 35 mpg highway 27 mpg city	Needs to hold six occupants comfortably	Needs to convert to all-wheel drive on the fly	Needs to cost under $40K	Must be available July	Must have superior exterior finishing
Engineering System						
• Develop conceptual definition	✔	✔	✔	✔	✔	✔
• Develop preliminary definition	✔	✔	✔	✔	✔	✔
• Produce product definition	✔	✔	✔	✔	✔	✔
• Certify product	✔				✔	
• Support product development						
• Manage project					✔	
Manufacturing System						
• Bid preparation						
• Program or contract start-up						
• Technical data preparation						
• Projection of first and subs	✔			✔	✔	✔
• Testing and commissioning					✔	
Customer Support						
• Product management						
• Manage customer						
• Contracts						
• Spares/tech pub/training				✔	✔	
• Maintenance engineering						
• Completion center				✔	✔	✔
• Aviation service						
Administrative Process						
• Finance/budget/billing						
• Human resources relations						
• Strategic plan and communication						

In this example matrix, it appears that the greatest area for opportunity to effect change is in the Engineering System. The team then could collect more detailed information about the individual cells within this matrix to help narrow the focus.

No matter the complexity of the product or process, these top-level tools assist the project champion and Black Belt in continually narrowing the focus. More detailed information about the individual cells within the matrix could be collected until the project is scoped to a manageable level. High-level process maps are created, followed by more detailed process maps as the input variables become more key and additional granularity is required. (Process maps are explained in more detail in a subsequent chapter in this book.)

Tip An important concept to remember is to avoid "drilling down" too quickly into the details of the process and stay at the highest process level possible for as long as possible.

At this point, the Black Belt still needs to determine where the greatest opportunity for improvement is in the process, by collecting more data about the individual process steps. Subsequently, the Black Belt will need to create a Cause & Effect (C&E) Matrix, as shown in the following figure. The numbers in the graphic correspond to the steps (on the next page) required to complete this matrix.

A C&E Matrix

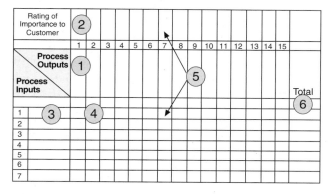

To complete this matrix:

1. The y's from the process identified from the previous CT Matrix are placed across the columns of the C&E Matrix.

2. The y's are ranked relative to one another on a scale of 1-10 with respect to their importance to the customer.

3. The process steps or CTXs obtained from the process mapping exercise are placed down the first column of the matrix, establishing the identity of each row. Depending on the number of process inputs, starting at a higher level (of process steps) is much more efficient.

4. The steps or CTXs are compared to the y's of the process by a force-ranking on the following (or similar) scale: 0, 1, 4, and 9. The forced ranking is done to prioritize the CTXs. In this step, the team should ask, "If a particular x was changed, would it significantly impact y, either positively or negatively?" If the team considers that the impact would be significant, then a ranking of 9 is given. If the team does not think the y will be impacted, then a score of 0 or 1 will be appropriate. If one person wants to give a ranking of 9 and the other team members want to give a ranking of 1, the team should not take the average, but should discuss the situation to determine what knowledge the person who wants to rank a 9 has that the other team members do not have.

5. For each row, the sum-product is calculated by multiplying the cell rating (from step 4) by the importance rating for the y in that column (from step 2). The products across each row are added together and stored in the last column, titled Totals (6).

6. The Totals column is then sorted in descending order. The values with the highest totals are those CTXs that are most likely to impact the project.

C&E Matrix Example:

A Black Belt was assigned to a team with the Engineering Systems process owners/representatives. Their goal was to apply the C&E Matrix to determine the initial "process" focus of a Black Belt project within the larger Engineering Systems process. To ensure that the team was cross-functional, the product development and management teams from each facet of the organization were also represented. The team started with previously created CT Trees and a CT Matrix. Each member had also conducted a review of the new product under development and reviewed data collected on previous new product introductions in their respective areas. They decided to create a C&E Matrix based on the current process performance and the relationship between customer requirements of this particular product and the Engineering Systems process steps.

The Team's C&E Matrix

Rating of Importance to Customer		6	9	9	10	10	7	
		1	2	3	4	5	6	
Process Inputs (Steps)		Needs to achieve 35 mpg highway 27 mpg city	Needs to hold six occupants comfortably	Needs to convert to all-wheel drive on the fly	Needs to cost under $40k	Must be available July 2003	Must have superior exterior finish	Total
2	Preliminary Design (D)	9	9	9	9	9	④	424
3	Product Definition - Optimize (O)	9	4	9	9	4	4	329
6	Manage Project	4	1	4	⑨	⑨	4	277
5	Support Production Development	4	4	4	4	1	⑨	209
1	Conceptual - Identify (I)	1	4	4	1	9	4	206
4	Certify Product - Validate (V)	4	1	4	4	4	1	156
Total Column Score		186	207	306	360	360	182	

CTSs were taken from the CT Matrix and placed along the top of the C&E Matrix. All six of these CTSs were then assigned a ranked score or rating from 1 to 10, based on the importance to the customer. The team noticed that these importance ratings received rankings from 6 through 10. The CT Matrix also identified the major process steps, 1 through 6, of the Engineering Systems process. (This served as their high-level process map.) These process steps then served as the process inputs down the left side of the matrix. Each step was ranked on the 0,1,4,9 scale to ascertain the linkage between the voice of the process (VOP), the process steps, and the voice of the customer (VOC) or CTSs. (The VOP are the "causes" and the VOC is the "effect"; hence the "C&E" Matrix.)

(To narrow the focus, another C&E Matrix was then created to link the customer requirements to the process steps. This is a mid-level application of the C&E Matrix because it is dealing with process steps vs. more-detailed process inputs from each step. Subsequent C&E Matrices can be created after one particular process or area is highlighted as having the greatest impact on the customer requirements.)

The team assessed the linkages based on collective experience and data. Considerations were based on existing and proposed process capability and technology roadmaps. For example, the "Preliminary Design Efforts" were scored lower (4) for "superior exterior finish" because this was an existing capability for the organization. The team was more concerned with maintaining exterior finish in the production process and therefore assigned a score of 9 to "Support Production Development." Also, the management team was much more concerned with managing total cost and schedule as it pertained to the "Manage Project" process step. Upon completion

©2002 GOAL/QPC,
Six Sigma Academy

of the rankings, the totals were calculated and the steps were sorted in descending order of the total scores.

A Pareto Chart was created based on the total scores for each process step, showing that the Preliminary Design step appeared to be the most critical step in the process, because it related to all of the customer requirements identified on the matrix. This process step contributes 26.5% of the total variation or risk to the development of this new product. Therefore, the first Black Belt project to be defined should concentrate efforts in this area.

A Pareto Chart
of the C&E Matrix Results

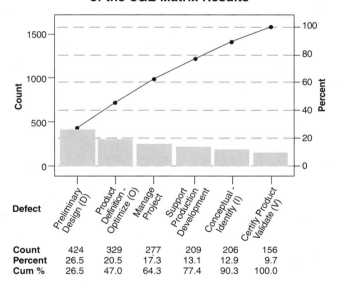

Defect	Preliminary Design (D)	Product Definition - Optimize (O)	Manage Project	Support Production Development	Conceptual - Identify (I)	Certify Product Validate (V)
Count	424	329	277	209	206	156
Percent	26.5	20.5	17.3	13.1	12.9	9.7
Cum %	26.5	47.0	64.3	77.4	90.3	100.0

A recommended cross-validation is to evaluate the total column scores in the matrix for each customer requirement. These scores are calculated similarly to the row totals. The column scores represent the weighted sums of the CTSs as they relate to the entire Engineering Systems process. Comparing these totals to the ratings assigned to their respective CTS ensures that the process gives fair weight and consideration to each of the customer requirements relative to the assigned ratings. A discrepancy would indicate either a significant disconnect in the process, unrealistic rankings of the process steps, or missing steps not included in the matrix. As an extreme example, a column totaling zero would indicate that none of the listed CTXs had any perceived effect on the CTY of that column.

Next Steps: Links to Other Tools

The team's next step would be to create a more detailed process map of the Preliminary Design process. The process map will include inputs and outputs of each detailed step. A subsequent C&E Matrix can then be conducted on the detailed process steps or process inputs from the detailed process map. The team will then evaluate the process inputs associated with these steps on an FMEA. The FMEA will be completed with the comprehensive list of inputs.

Links to Other Tools

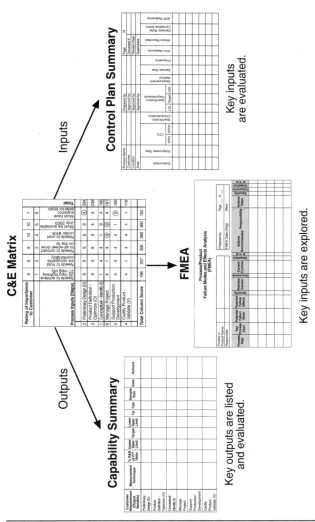

C&E Matrix

Control Plan Summary

Inputs

Key inputs
are evaluated.

FMEA

Key inputs are explored.

Outputs

Capability Summary

Key outputs are listed
and evaluated.

Each tool is applied with greater granularity until the potential critical inputs or x's are identified. The results of the C&E Matrix exercise are used in the FMEA exercise. The team will strategically "drill down" into the various levels of the process, from the complex level down to the element level. The CTXs that are identified as having high values in the CT Matrix are the potential critical x's. Data should be collected around these x's to validate their significance.

The process output variables from the C&E Matrix should drive additional action to complete capability studies on the y's, including measurement system analysis. (Measurement systems analysis is discussed in greater detail in a subsequent chapter of this book.) For every input that has a high impact on the CTYs of interest on the C&E matrix and/or FMEA, an initial control plan could be developed; subsequent action on capabilities on the x's may be postponed until the completion of the FMEA.

 **Basic Statistics**

Why use it?

Once facts or data have been classified and summarized, they must be interpreted, presented, or communicated in an efficient manner to drive data-based decisions. Statistical problem-solving methods are used to determine if processes are on target, if the total variability is small compared to specifications, and if the process is stable over time. Businesses can no longer afford to make decisions based on averages alone; process variations and their sources must be identified and eliminated.

What does it do?

The Measure Phase involves designing data collection plans, collecting data, and then using that data to describe the process.

Descriptive statistics are used to describe or summarize a specific collection of data (typically samples of data). Descriptive statistics encompass both numerical and graphical techniques, and are used to determine the:

- Central tendency of the data.
- Spread or dispersion of the data.
- Symmetry and skewness of the data.

Inferential statistics is the method of collecting samples of data and making inferences about population parameters from the sample data.

Before reviewing basic statistics, the different types of data must be identified. The type of data that has been collected as process inputs (x's) and / or outputs (y's) will determine the type of statistics or analysis that can be performed.

Selecting Statistical Techniques

Outputs

		Attribute	Variable
Inputs	Attribute	Proportion tests, Chi-square	t-test, ANOVA, DOE, Regression
	Variable	Discriminant analysis, Logistic regression	Correlation, Multiple regression

The two classifications of data types are variable or attribute. Another way to classify data is as discrete or continuous.

Continuous data:

- Has no boundaries between adjoining values.
- Includes most non-counting intervals and ratios (e.g., time).

Discrete data:

- Has clear boundaries.
- Includes nominals, counts, and rank-orders, (e.g., Monday vs. Friday, an electrical circuit with or without a short).

Data Type Classifications

	Variable	Variable Binary	Attribute Binary	Attribute > 2 Categories
Discrete	Ordinal or rank-orders that get treated as an interval scale (i.e., day of week, hour of the day, age in years, counts (integers), income, proportions)	Binary with a value rank or order (i.e.,good/ bad, on-time/not on-time, pass/fail)	Binary with-out a value rank (i.e., male/ female, heads/tails coin toss)	Nominal or categorical (i.e., phone numbers, primary colors, eye color, method A,B,C, or D)
Continuous	Ratio and interval-type data (i.e.,temperature scale, weight, length, time, wavelength)		Cannot exist	

Black Belts should strive to collect continuous, variable data to enable straightforward descriptive and inferential statistics.

How do I do it? 🏃

Measures of Central Tendency

There are three measures of central tendency: the mean, the median, and the mode.

- The *mean* (μ) is the average of a set of values. The mean of a population can be calculated using the formula:

$$\mu = \frac{\sum\limits_{i=1}^{N} x_i}{N} = \frac{x_1 + x_2 + x_3 + \ldots + x_N}{N}$$

N = total number of data points in the population

$$\sum\limits_{i=1}^{N} = \text{Sum all values from the first to last}$$

Examples:

Average Days Late: $\dfrac{1 + 2 + 3 + 4 + 5}{5} = 3.0$

Inspection (Pass/Fail): $\dfrac{0 + 0 + 1 + 1}{4} = 0.5$

- The *median* is the midpoint in a string of sorted data, where 50% of the observations or values are below and 50% are above. If there are an even number of observations, it is the average of the two middle numbers.

Tip Order the data from low to high values when determining the median. This will make it easier to select the middle observation.

Examples:
For the odd number of observations 1, 2, 3, 4, 5, 6, 7, the median is 4. For the even number of observations 1, 2, 3, 4, 5, 6, 7, 8, the median is 4.5.

• The *mode* is the most frequently occurring value in a data set. For example, in the data set 1, 2, 3, 3, 5, 7, 9, the mode is 3.

Measures of Spread

Measures of spread include the range, the deviation, the variance, and the standard deviation.

• The *range* is the difference between the largest and smallest observations in a data set.

Range = maximum observation − minimum observation

For the data set 1,2,3,3,5,7,9, the range is 9-1 = 8.

• The *deviation* is the distance between a data point and the mean.

Deviation = $(X-\mu)$

In the example 1,2,3,3,5,7,9, the mean is $(1+2+3+3+5+7+9)/7 = 30/7 = 4.29$, and the deviation of the data point 9 is $(9 - 4.29) = 4.71$.

• The *variance* is the average squared deviation about the mean. The squared deviation of a single point is calculated by subtracting it from the mean and squaring the difference.

• The *standard deviation* is the square root of the average squared deviation about the mean (i.e., the square root of the variance). The standard deviation is the most commonly used measurement

---

to quantify variability and will be in the same units as the data collected. The formula to calculate the standard deviation in a population is:

$$\sigma = \sqrt{\frac{\displaystyle\sum_{i=1}^{N}(x_i - \mu)^2}{N}}$$

To determine the population standard deviation for the data set 1, 2, 3:

X	μ	X − μ	(X − μ)²
1	2	− 1	1
2	2	0	0
3	2	1	1
Σ = 6			2
N = 3			
μ = 2			

$$\sigma = \sqrt{\frac{\displaystyle\sum_{i=1}^{N}(x_i - \mu)^2}{N}}$$

$$\sigma = \sqrt{\frac{(1-2)^2 + (2-2)^2 + (3-2)^2}{3}}$$

$$\sigma = \sqrt{0.667} = 0.8167$$

The variance for a sum of two independent variables is found by adding both variances. The standard deviation for the total is the square root of the sum of both variances.

If σ_1^2 = variance of variable 1, and

σ_2^2 = variance of variable 2, then

$\sigma_T^2 = \sigma_1^2 + \sigma_2^2$ and

$\sigma_T = \sqrt{\sigma_1^2 + \sigma_2^2}$

Population vs. Sample

A population is every possible observation or census, but it is very rare to capture the entire population in data collection. Instead, samples, or subsets of populations as illustrated in the following figure, are captured.

Populations and Samples

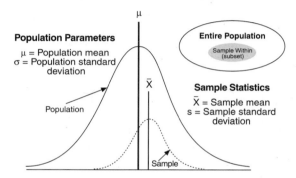

A statistic, by definition, is a number that describes a sample characteristic. Information from samples can be used to "infer" or approximate a population characteristic called a parameter. (More information about using samples to infer population parameters can be found in the chapter on confidence intervals in this book.)

Sample Statistics Approximate the Population Parameters

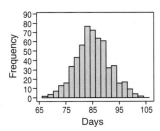 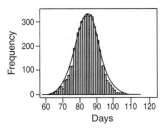

Sample Statistics	Population Parameters
$\overline{X}$ = 84.99	μ = 85.06
s^2 = 34.57	σ^2 = 36.53
s = 5.88	σ = 6.04
n = 600	N = 5,000

Data is obtained using samples because the entire population may not be known or may be too expensive to measure. Descriptive statistics can apply to any sample or population; however, the equations are unique for each.

Population And Sample Equations

Sample mean
n = A subset of the population

$$\overline{X} = \frac{\sum\limits_{i=1}^{n} x_i}{n} = \frac{x_1 + x_2 + x_3 + \ldots + x_n}{n}$$

Sample standard deviation

$$s = \sqrt{\frac{\sum\limits_{i=1}^{n} (x_i - \bar{x})^2}{(n-1)}}$$

Population mean
N = Every member of the population

$$\mu = \frac{\sum\limits_{i=1}^{N} x_i}{N} = \frac{x_1 + x_2 + x_3 + \ldots + x_N}{N}$$

Population standard deviation

$$\sigma = \sqrt{\frac{\sum\limits_{i=1}^{N} (x_i - \mu)^2}{N}}$$

Properties of a Normal Distribution

A normal distribution can be described by its mean and standard deviation. The standard normal distribution is a special case of the normal distribution and has a mean of zero and a standard deviation of one. The tails of the distribution extend to ± infinity. The area under the curve represents 100% of the possible observations. The curve is symmetrical such that each side of the mean has the same shape and contains 50% of the total area. Theoretically, about 95% of the population is contained within ± 2 standard deviations.

The Standard Normal Curve

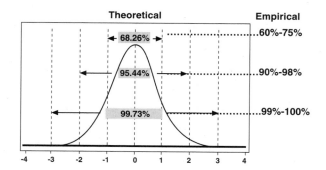

©2002 GOAL/QPC,
Six Sigma Academy

If a data set is normally distributed, then the standard deviation and mean can be used to determine the percentage (or probability) of observations within a selected range. Any normally distributed scale can be transformed to its equivalent Z scale or score using the formula:

$$Z = (x - \mu)/\sigma$$

x will often represent a lower specification limit (LSL) or upper specification limit (USL). Z, the "sigma value," is a measure of standard deviations from the mean.

Any normal data distribution can be transformed to a standard normal curve using the Z transformation. The area under the curve is used to predict the probability of an event occurring.

Z Transformations

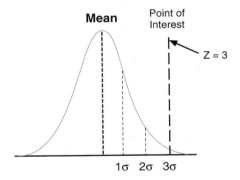

Example:

If the mean is 85 days and the standard deviation is five days, what would be the yield if the USL is 90 days?

Using The Z-Transform To Predict Yield

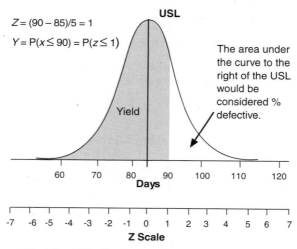

$Z = (90 - 85)/5 = 1$

$Y = P(x \leq 90) = P(z \leq 1)$

USL

The area under the curve to the right of the USL would be considered % defective.

Yield

Days

60   70   80   90   100   110   120

Z Scale

-7 -6 -5 -4 -3 -2 -1 0 1 2 3 4 5 6 7

$P(z < 1) = 1 - P(z > 1) = 1 - 0.15865 = 0.8413$ Yield $\cong$ 84.1%

A standard Z table is used to determine the area under the curve. The area under the curve represents probability.

Note: A standard Z table can be found in the Appendix of this book. This particular table provides probabilities on the left side. When using other tables, verify which probability it is providing. Tables may accumulate area under the curve from the left or right tail. Graphically depicting the problem statement and practical interpretation of the results is recommended.

Because the curve is symmetric, the area shown as yield would be 1-P(z>1) = 0.841 or 84.1%.

In accordance with the equation, Z can be calculated for any "point of interest," x.

Variation

The following figure shows three normal distributions with the same mean. What differs between the distributions is the variation.

Three Normal Distributions

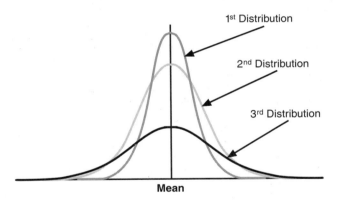

The first distribution displays less variation or dispersion about the mean. The second distribution displays more variation and would have a greater standard deviation. The third distribution displays even more variation.

Short-term vs. Long-term Variation

The duration over which data is collected will determine whether short-term or long-term variation has been captured within the subgroup.

There are two types of variation in every process: *common cause variation* and *special cause variation.* Common cause variation is completely random (i.e., the next data point's specific value cannot be predicted). It is the natural variation of the process. Special cause variation is the nonrandom variation in the process. It is the result of an event, an action, or a series of events or actions. The nature and causes of special cause variation are different for every process.

Short-term data is data that is collected from the process in subgroups. Each subgroup is collected over a short length of time to capture common cause variation only (i.e., data is not collected across different shifts because variation can exist from operator to operator). Thus, the subgroup consists of "like" things collected over a narrow time frame and is considered a "snapshot in time" of the process. For example, a process may use several raw material lots per shift. A representative short-term sample may consist of CTQ measurements within one lot.

Long-term data is considered to contain both special and common causes of variation that are typically observed when all of the input variables have varied over their full range. To continue with the same example, long-term data would consist of several raw material lots measured across several short-term samples.

Process Variation Over Time

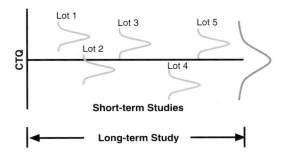

Processes tend to exhibit more variation in the long term than in the short term. Long-term variability is made up of short-term variability and process drift. The shift from short term to long term can be quantified by taking both short-term and long-term samples.

Long-term Drift

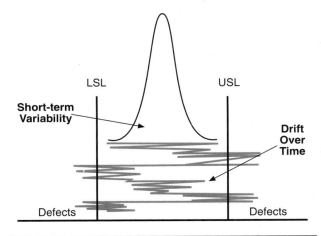

On average, short-term process means tend to shift and drift by 1.5 sigmas.

$$Z_{lt} = Z_{st} - 1.5$$

(The short-term Z (Z_{st}) is also known as the benchmark sigma value. The Rolled Throughput Yield (RTY) section of this book discusses several related Six Sigma metrics used to evaluate processes.)

A Six Sigma process would have six standard deviations between the mean and the closest specification limit for a short-term capability study. The following figure illustrates the Z-score relationship to the Six Sigma philosophy:

**Z-Score Relationship
To Six Sigma Philosophy**

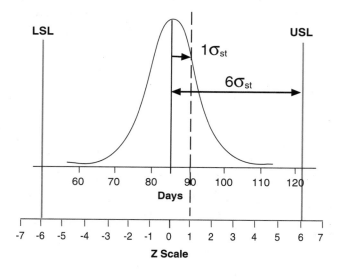

In a Six Sigma process, customer satisfaction and business objectives are robust to shifts caused by process or product variation.

Six Sigma as a Statistical Measure

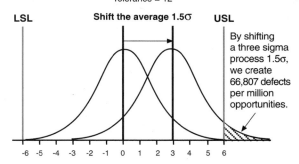

Three Sigma Process
Average = 0
St. Dev. = 2
Tolerance = 12

LSL   Shift the average 1.5σ   USL

By shifting a three sigma process 1.5σ, we create 66,807 defects per million opportunities.

-6 -5 -4 -3 -2 -1 0 1 2 3 4 5 6

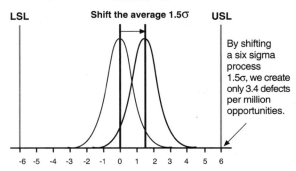

Six Sigma Process
Average = 0
St. Dev. = 1
Tolerance = 12

LSL   Shift the average 1.5σ   USL

By shifting a six sigma process 1.5σ, we create only 3.4 defects per million opportunities.

-6 -5 -4 -3 -2 -1 0 1 2 3 4 5 6

DPMO is directly related to Z. A reference chart to convert from Z_{lt} to DPMO can be found in the Appendix of this book. This chart already includes the 1.5 sigma shift. For example, shifting a Six Sigma process 1.5 sigma creates 3.4 defects per million opportunities. Recall our previous example with a $Z_{st} = 1.0$. If so, then $Z_{lt} = 1.0 - 1.5 = -0.5$. From the conversion table, the long-term DPMO is 691,500 or 69.15% defects. The yield is $(1-0.6915) = 0.3085$ or 30.85%.

©2002 GOAL/QPC,
Six Sigma Academy

 **Process Maps**

SIPOC

Why use it?

SIPOC is used to document a process at a high level and visually show the process, from suppliers' inputs to the products or services received by customers. The name comes from the column headings on a SIPOC chart: **S**uppliers, **I**nputs, **P**rocess, **O**utputs, and **C**ustomers.

What does it do?

SIPOC:

- Identifies process boundaries.
- Identifies the customers and suppliers of a process.
- Identifies the process inputs supplied by the suppliers and the process outputs used by the customer.
- Helps in identifying data collection needs.

Components of a SIPOC

- A *process description* is an explanation of a process that provides outputs to meet the needs of customers.
- The *input and output boundaries* define the start and stop boundaries of the process.
- The *outputs* are the "results" of the process. Special care should be taken to determine how these outputs relate to the customers' expectations (CTSs) (i.e., do they meet or exceed the customer requirements?).
- The *customers* are the people who receive and put requirements on the outputs. Customers can be either internal or external; the SIPOC chart should be specific in documenting which.

- *Customer requirements and measures* are the quantifiable expectations of the process outputs. The output must be measured and then compared to customer requirements to quantify customer satisfaction.

- The *inputs* are what the process needs to function.

- The *input requirements and measures* are the quantifiable expectations the process puts on the inputs. For a process to create outputs that meet the customer requirements, it must have inputs that meet specific requirements. The SIPOC should document what the process requires of the inputs that are received before the start of the process.

- The *suppliers* provide the necessary inputs to the process. The SIPOC should be as specific as possible in documenting supplier information. For example, if a supplier is internal, the SIPOC should list the function and point of contact for the particular process input.

How do I do it?

The following figure shows the steps in creating a SIPOC. The numbers in the graphic correspond to the numbers of the steps that follow.

Creating a SIPOC

S	I	P	O	C
Suppliers	**Inputs**	**Process**	**Outputs**	**Customers**
Providers of the process	Inputs into the process	Top-level process description	Outputs of the process	Receivers of the process outputs
		Start ②		
⑥	⑤	①	③	④
		End ②		

1. Provide a description of the process.

2. Define the start and end of the process that the project is focused on.

3. List the outputs of the process.
   - Requirements of the outputs should also be listed, as well as how requirements will be measured.

4. List the customers of each process output.

5. List the inputs required for the process, as well as how these inputs will be measured.
   - The quantifiable expectations of the process should also be listed.

6. List the suppliers of the process.

A SIPOC for a
Lecture Development Process

S	I	P	O	C
Suppliers	**Inputs**	**Process**	**Outputs**	**Customers**
Subject expert	Class objectives	Start: Need for lecture development identified	Class outline	Department head
Department head	Class subject			
University	Teaching guidelines	Develop class lecture	Lecture developed in two weeks	Department head, teacher
Department head	Subject expert			
Department head	Target time per lecture (50+/-5 min.)		Reviews	Subject expert
Department head	Reviewers	End: Lecture materials printed	Printed materials	Lecturer
Printing company	Printing service			

Process Mapping

Why use it?

Process mapping identifies the flow of events in a process as well as the inputs (x's) and outputs (y's) in each step of a process.

What does it do?

Process mapping:

- Graphically identifies the steps in a process.

- Visually shows the complexity of a process and identifies sources of non-value-added activities (i.e., rework loops and redundancy in a process).

- Identifies the key process input variables (x's) that go into a process step and the resultant key output variables (y's).

- Classifies all input variables (x's) to a process step as noise, controllable factors, or standard operating procedures (SOP).

- Builds on the Flowchart tool by adding more process information.

Components of a Process Map

- The *inputs* (x's) are the key process variables that are required to perform a process step. Inputs could be anything in the categories of people, methods, materials, machinery, measurements, or environment.

- The *process steps* are the tasks that transform the inputs of the process into the outputs of the process.

- The *outputs* (y's) are the key variables resulting from the performance of the process step. Outputs can be goods, services, measurements, or consequences.

A Process Map

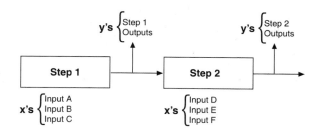

How do I do it?

1. **Define the scope of the process.**

   • Clearly define where the process starts and stops. These are the process boundaries.

   • Process maps can be done at different levels such as an overall level, operation level, or micro-task level. The team should decide which level is appropriate.

   • The process scope can be defined with a SIPOC.

2. **Document all the steps in the process.**

   • To do this correctly, "walk through" the process by pretending to be the product or service being operated on. Document all the steps of the as-is process, not the should-be process. Activities are shown as a rectangle on a process map.

   • Document the decision points. Decision points must pose a question. The response to the question will lead to multiple paths. Decision points are shown as a diamond on a process map.

3. **List all outputs (y's) at each process step.**

4. **List all inputs (x's) at each process step.**

5. **Classify all inputs (x's) as:**

   - Controllable (C): Inputs that can be changed to see the effect on the output (y). Examples are speed or feed rate on a machine, temperature or pressure in a thermodynamic process, or document type or batch size in a transactional process.

   - Standard operating procedures (S): Standard methods or procedures for running the process. Examples are cleaning, safety, and loading of components in an industrial process, and training, calling method, or data entry items in a transactional process.

   - Noise (N): Things that cannot or that have been chosen not to be controlled due to cost or difficulty. Examples are ambient temperature or humidity in an industrial process, or computer network or operator in a transactional process.

6. **As applicable, list the operating specification and process targets for controllable inputs.**

   - For the controllable inputs that have these targets, list the target input and the specified lower and/or upper limits on the setting.

Class Lecture Development Process Map

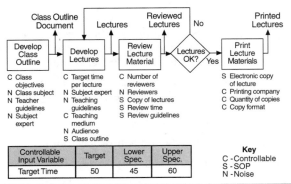

Controllable Input Variable	Target	Lower Spec.	Upper Spec.
Target Time	50	45	60

Key
C - Controllable
S - SOP
N - Noise

©2002 GOAL/QPC,
Six Sigma Academy

Rolled Throughput Yield

Why use it?

Rolled Throughput Yield (RTY) is used to assess the true yield of a process that includes a hidden factory. A hidden factory adds no value to the customer and involves fixing things that weren't done right the first time.

What does it do?

RTY determines the probability of a product or service making it through a multistep process without being scrapped or ever reworked.

How do I do it?

There are two methods to measure RTY:

Method 1 assesses defects per unit (dpu), when all that is known is the final number of units produced and the number of defects.

- A *defect* is defined as something that does not conform to a known and accepted customer standard.

- A *unit* is the product, information, or service used or purchased by a customer.

- An *opportunity for a defect* is a measured characteristic on a unit that needs to conform to a customer standard (e.g., the ohms of an electrical resistor, the diameter of a pen, the time it takes to deliver a package, or the address field on a form).

- *Defective* is when the entire unit is deemed unacceptable because of the nonconformance of any one of the opportunities for a defect.

Shown in the following diagram are six units, each containing five opportunities for a defect.

Opportunities for a Defect

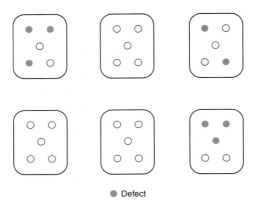

● Defect

Given that any one defect can cause a unit to be defective, it appears the yield of this process is 50%. This, however, is not the whole story. Assuming that defects are randomly distributed, the special form of the Poisson distribution formula

$$RTY = e^{-dpu}$$

can be used to estimate the number of units with zero defects (i.e., the RTY).

The previous *figure* showed eight defects over six units, resulting in 1.33 dpu. Entering this into our formula:

$$RTY = e^{-1.33}$$

$$RTY = 0.264$$

According to this calculation, this process can expect an average of 26.4% defect-free units that have not been reworked (which is much different than the assumed 50%).

Method 2 determines throughput yield (Y_{tp}), when the specific yields at each opportunity for a defect are known.

If, on a unit, the yield at each opportunity for a defect is known (i.e., the five yields at each opportunity in the previous figure), then these yields can be multiplied together to determine the RTY. The yields at each opportunity for a defect are known as the throughput yields, which can be calculated as

$$Y_{tp} = e^{-dpu}$$

for that specific opportunity for a defect for attribute data, and

$$Y_{tp} = 1 - P(\text{defect})$$

for variable data, where $P(\text{defect})$ is the probability of a defect based on the normal distribution.

Shown in the following figure is one unit from the previous figure in which the associated Y_{tp}'s at each opportunity were measured for many units.

Throughput Yield
at Each Opportunity for a Defect

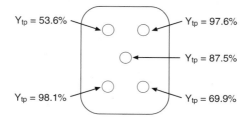

$Y_{tp} = 53.6\%$

$Y_{tp} = 97.6\%$

$Y_{tp} = 87.5\%$

$Y_{tp} = 98.1\%$

$Y_{tp} = 69.9\%$

Multiplying these yields together results in the RTY:

$$RTY = Y_{tp1} \times Y_{tp2} \times Y_{tp3} \times Y_{tp4} \times Y_{tp5}$$

$$RTY = 0.536 \times 0.976 \times 0.875 \times 0.981 \times 0.699$$

$$RTY = 0.314$$

According to this calculation, an average of 31.4% defect-free units that have not been reworked can be expected.

Defects Per Million Opportunities

Why use it?

Defects per million opportunities (DPMO) helps to determine the capability of a process.

What does it do?

DPMO allows for the calculation of capability at one or more opportunities and ultimately, if desired, for the entire organization.

How do I do it?

Calculating DPMO depends on whether the data is variable or attribute, and if there is one or more than one opportunity for a defect.

If there is:

- *One opportunity with variable data,* use the Z transform to determine the probability of observing a defect, then multiply by 1 million.

- *One opportunity with attribute data,* calculate the percent defects, then multiple by 1 million.

- *More than one opportunity with both variable and/or attribute data,* use one of two methods to determine DPMO.

1. **Calculate the total defects per opportunity (DPO).**

   - To calculate DPO, sum the defects and sum the total opportunities for a defect, then divide the defects by the total opportunities and multiply by 1 million.

   Example:

   If there are eight defects and thirty total opportunities for a defect, then

   $$DPMO = (8/30) \times 1,000,000 = 266,667$$

   - When using this method to evaluate multiple opportunity variable data, convert the calculated DPMO into defects and opportunities for each variable, then sum them to get total defects and opportunities.

   Example:

   If one step in a process has a DPMO of 50,000 and another step has a DPMO of 100,000, there are 150,000 total defects for 2 million opportunities or 75,000 DPMO overall.

2. **Calculate the average yield per opportunity, also known as the normalized yield (Y_{na}).**

   - To calculate Y_{na} from RTY, assuming there are m opportunities per unit, take RTY to the 1/m power.

   $$Y_{na} = RTY^{(1/m)}$$

   To calculate RTY from Y_{na}, take Y_{na} to the mth power.

   $$RTY = Y_{na}{}^{m}$$

   $$DPMO = (1-Y_{na}) \times 1,000,000$$

Example:

If there are five opportunities per unit and the RTY is 0.264, then:

$$Y_{na} = 0.264^{(1/5)}$$

$$Y_{na} = 0.766$$

$$DPMO = (1 - 0.766) \times 1{,}000{,}000 = 234{,}000$$

The difference between DPO and Y_{na} is that Y_{na} is an estimate based on the Poisson distribution, and DPO is an actual calculation. As the defect rate falls below 10%, these values converge.

⚡ Sigma Values

Why use it?

Sigma values are calculated to determine a baseline for an opportunity, process, or product. Sigma values can also be used to fairly compare different products, services, information, or divisions within a organization and, if desired, benchmark the like.

Note: Sigma has many different definitions and can be used in many different ways:

- As a benchmark.

- As a population's standard deviation.

- As a baseline measure that describes how far a process mean is from the nearest specification.

- As a measure of distance (e.g., two process means are 4.5 sigma apart).

What does it do?

Sigma helps establish baselines and set targets, goals, and objectives against which progress can be measured.

How do I do it? 🏃

Once DPMO has been calculated, sigma values can be looked up in a table. Tables may be found in many common computer software packages and in appendices of statistical books. Remember that it is necessary to understand whether the data collected is short term or long term, as it may be necessary to either add or subtract 1.5 to the lookup value.

Partial DPMO to Z Table

DPMO	N	DPMO	N	DPMO	N	DPMO	N	DPMO	N
500000	0.000	95000	1.311	2500	2.807	480	3.302	75	3.791
480000	0.050	90000	1.341	2400	2.820	460	3.314	70	3.808
460000	0.100	85000	1.372	2300	2.834	440	3.326	65	3.826
440000	0.151	80000	1.405	2200	2.848	420	3.339	60	3.846
420000	0.202	75000	1.440	2100	2.863	400	3.353	55	3.867
400000	0.253	70000	1.476	2000	2.878	380	3.367	50	3.891
380000	0.305	65000	1.514	1900	2.894	360	3.382	45	3.916
360000	0.358	60000	1.555	1800	2.911	340	3.398	40	3.944
340000	0.412	55000	1.598	1700	2.929	320	3.414	35	3.976
320000	0.468	50000	1.645	1600	2.948	300	3.432	30	4.013
300000	0.524	45000	1.695	1500	2.968	280	3.450	25	4.056
280000	0.583	40000	1.751	1400	2.989	260	3.470	20	4.107
260000	0.643	35000	1.812	1300	3.011	240	3.492	15	4.173
240000	0.706	30000	1.881	1200	3.036	220	3.515	10	4.265
220000	0.772	25000	1.960	1100	3.062	200	3.540	5	4.417
200000	0.842	20000	2.054	1000	3.090	180	3.568	4	4.465
180000	0.915	15000	2.170	900	3.121	160	3.599	3	4.526
160000	0.994	10000	2.326	800	3.156	140	3.633	2	4.611
140000	1.080	5000	2.576	700	3.195	120	3.673	1	4.753
120000	1.175	4000	2.652	600	3.239	100	3.719	0.5	4.892
100000	1.282	3000	2.748	500	3.291	80	3.775	0.1	5.199

Not Shifted: Long-term DPMO will give long-term Z.

Short-term data is considered free of special causes. For example, data collected over one shift does not allow any special causes due to differences in shift. In a transactional process, short-term data could measure one administrator over one day.

Long-term data is considered to contain both special and random cause variation, typically observed when the input variables have varied over their full range.

Processes tend to exhibit more variation in the long term than the short term. Shown below is a process in which subgroups of data were collected on a daily basis (small bell curves) for an extended period of time. The shifting and drifting of the subgroup averages (the shift factor) is due to many factors such as tool wear, different operators working the process, different lots of raw materials, etc. It has been demonstrated that because of these many causes, the subgroup means tend to shift and drift, on average, 1.5 standard deviations.

Subgroup Drift

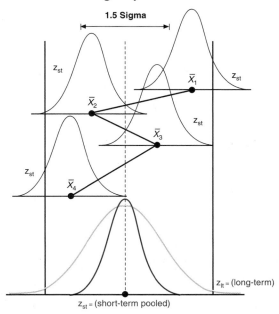

How do I practically use the shift factor?

If short-term data has been collected, then the calculation will be to baseline a process to determine a short-term sigma (Z_{st}). If long-term data is not available but long-term performance needs to be estimated, then 1.5 can be subtracted from the Z_{st} to estimate long-term performance. (The opposite also is true: to estimate short-term performance, add 1.5 to the Z_{lt}.)

Using the Shift Factor

To know:

		Z_{st}	Z_{lt}
		Short-term capability	Long-term capability
With data collected:	Z_{st} Short-term data	✔	Subtract 1.5
	Z_{lt} Long-term data	Add 1.5	✔

$$Z_{lt} = Z_{st} - 1.5$$

Note: Use 1.5 as the shift factor until enough data on the process has been collected to distinguish between long-term and short-term variation. Once enough data has been collected, the exact shift factor for the process can then be determined, although it is difficult and data intensive to do so when using attribute data.

Example:

A DPMO of 266,667 was calculated in the previous chapter. If we consider it to be long-term data, looking up the sigma value in a table shows a long-term sigma value of 0.62. Considering the need to report a short-term sigma value, we can add 1.5 to the sigma value to obtain a short-term sigma value of 2.12.

---

64 Sigma Values

©2002 GOAL/QPC,
Six Sigma Academy

Cause & Effect/ Fishbone Diagram

Why use it?

Cause & Effect (C&E) Diagrams allow a team to identify, explore, and graphically display, in increasing detail, important possible causes related to a problem or condition to discover its root cause(s).

What does it do?

A C&E Diagram:

- Enables a team to focus on the content of the problem, not on the history of the problem or differing personal interests of team members.

- Creates a snapshot of the collective knowledge and consensus of a team around a problem. This builds support for the resulting solutions.

- Focuses the team on causes, not symptoms.

How do I do it?

1. **Select the most appropriate Cause & Effect format.**

   There are two major formats:

   - A *dispersion analysis type* is constructed by placing individual causes within each "major" cause category and then asking of each individual cause "Why does this cause (dispersion) happen?" This question is repeated for the next level of detail until the team runs out of causes. (The graphic examples shown in step 3 of this section are based on this format.)

- A *process classification type* uses the major steps of the process in place of the major cause categories. The root cause questioning process is the same as the dispersion analysis type.

2. **Generate the causes needed to build a Cause & Effect Diagram, using either:**

   - Brainstorming without previous preparation.

   - Check Sheets based on data collected by team members before the meeting.

3. **Construct the Cause & Effect/Fishbone Diagram.**

   a) Place the problem statement in a box on the righthand side of the writing surface.

   - Allow plenty of space. Use a flipchart sheet, butcher paper, or a large white board. A paper surface is preferred because the final Cause & Effect Diagram can be moved.

Causes
"Bones"
(Major cause categories)

Effect

Late pizza deliveries on Fridays & Saturdays

Tip Make sure everyone agrees on the problem statement. Include as much information as possible on the "what," "where," "when," and "how much" of the problem. Use data to specify the problem.

©2002 GOAL/QPC,
Six Sigma Academy

b) Draw major cause categories or steps in the production or service process. Connect them to the "backbone" of the fishbone chart.

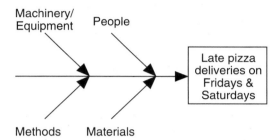

Illustration Note: In a process classification type format, replace the major "bone" categories with: "Order Taking," "Preparation," "Cooking," and "Delivery."

• Be flexible in the major cause "bones" that are used. For a *Production Process* the traditional categories are: Machines (equipment), Methods (how work is done), Materials (components or raw materials), and People (the human element). For a *Service Process* the traditional methods are: Policies (higher-level decision rules), Procedures (steps in a task), Plant (equipment and space), and People. In both types of processes, Environment (buildings, logistics, humidity, temperature, and space), and Measurement (calibration and data collection) are also frequently used. *There is no perfect set or number of categories. Make them fit the problem.*

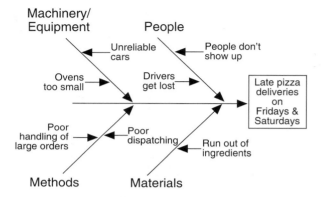

Machinery/
Equipment
People

Unreliable cars
People don't show up

Ovens too small
Drivers get lost

Late pizza deliveries on Fridays & Saturdays

Poor handling of large orders
Poor dispatching
Run out of ingredients

Methods
Materials

c) Place the brainstormed or data-based causes in the appropriate category.

• In brainstorming, possible causes can be placed in a major cause category as each is generated, or only after the entire list has been created. Either works well but brainstorming the whole list first maintains the creative flow of ideas without being constrained by the major cause categories or where the ideas fit in each "bone."

• Some causes seem to fit in more than one category. Ideally each cause should be in only one category, but some of the "people" causes may legitimately belong in two places. Place them in both categories and see how they work out in the end.

Tip If ideas are slow in coming, use the major cause categories as catalysts (e.g., "What in 'materials' is causing . . . ?").

d) Ask repeatedly of each cause listed on the "bones," either:

• "Why does it happen?" For example, under "Run out of ingredients," this question would lead to

©2002 GOAL/QPC,
Six Sigma Academy

more basic causes such as "Inaccurate ordering,"
"Poor use of space," and so on.

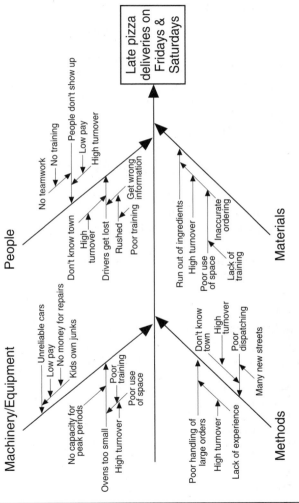

- "What could happen?" For example, under "Run out of ingredients," this question would lead to a deeper understanding of the problem such as "Boxes," "Prepared dough," "Toppings," and so on.

Tip For each deeper cause, continue to push for deeper understanding, but know when to stop. A rule of thumb is to stop questioning when a cause is controlled by more than one level of management removed from the group. Otherwise, the process could become an exercise in frustration. Use common sense.

e) Interpret or test for root cause(s) by one or more of the following:

- Look for causes that appear repeatedly within or across major cause categories.

- Select through either an unstructured consensus process or one that is structured, such as Nominal Group Technique or Multivoting.

- Gather data through Check Sheets or other formats to determine the relative frequencies of the different causes.

Variations

Traditionally, Cause & Effect Diagrams have been created in a meeting setting. The completed "fishbone" is often reviewed by others and/or confirmed with data collection. An effective alternative is to prominently display a large, highly visible, blank fishbone chart in a work area. Everyone posts both potential causes and solutions on Post-it™ Notes in each of the categories. Causes and solutions are reviewed, tested, and posted. This technique opens up the process to the knowledge and creativity of every person in the operation.

Bed Assignment Delay

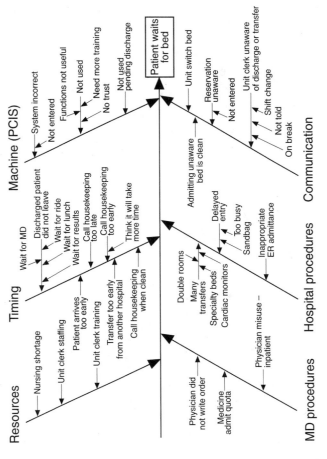

Patient waits for bed

Machine (PCIS)
- System incorrect
- Not entered
- Functions not useful
- Not used
  - Need more training
  - No trust
- Not used pending discharge

Communication
- Unit switch bed
- Reservation unaware
- Not entered
- Unit clerk unaware of discharge or transfer
  - Shift change
  - Not told
  - On break

Timing
- Wait for MD
- Discharged patient did not leave
- Wait for ride
- Wait for lunch
- Wait for results
- Call housekeeping too late
- Call housekeeping too early
- Think it will take more time

Hospital procedures
- Admitting unaware bed is clean
- Delayed entry
  - Too busy
  - Sandbag
- Inappropriate ER admittance

Resources
- Nursing shortage
- Unit clerk staffing
- Patient arrives too early
- Unit clerk training
- Transfer too early from another hospital
- Call housekeeping when clean

MD procedures
- Double rooms
- Many transfers
- Specialty beds
- Cardiac monitors
- Physician misuse – inpatient
- Physician did not write order
- Medicine admit quota

*Information provided courtesy of
Rush-Presbyterian-St. Luke's Medical Center*

Causes for Bent Pins (Plug-In Side)

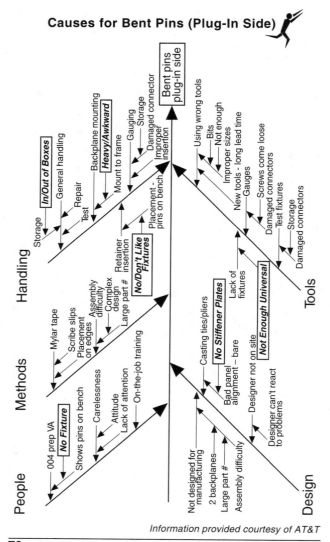

Information provided courtesy of AT&T

Measurement Systems Analysis

Why use it?

Measurement systems, if not functioning properly, can be a source of variability that can negatively impact capability. If measurement is a source of variability, organizations can be rejecting good units and/or accepting bad units. Therefore, it must be determined if the measurement system is reliable before the baseline capability can be determined. Doing so allows the organization to properly accept good units and properly reject bad units, thus establishing the true quality level.

What does it do?

Measurement systems analysis (MSA) is a series of designed tests that allows an organization to determine whether their measurement system is reliable. There are two types of MSAs; the choice of which one to use depends on whether the data is variable or attribute.

Variable Data

For variable data, the measurement system is comprised of the units being measured, the gauge, and the operators and their methods. The tree diagram on the next page shows the relationship of the sources of variation.

Sources of Variation

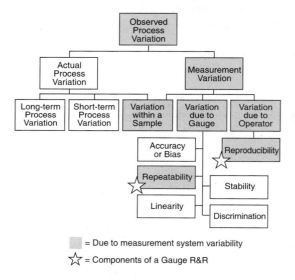

= Due to measurement system variability

☆ = Components of a Gauge R&R

When conducting an MSA, the organization must evaluate the bias, linearity, stability, discrimination, and variability (or precision) in the measurement system.

The *bias* is the difference between the observed average value of measurements and a known standard or master value. If bias exists in the average measured value, the measurement system may require calibration.

The *linearity* determines whether a bias exists in the measurement system over its operating range. For example, thermometers or scales may be biased when measuring at the low end of the scale, if the instruments are intended for larger values of measure.

The *stability* determines the measurement system's ability to measure consistently over time such that the measurement system does not drift.

The *discrimination* or resolution of the measurement system is the ability to detect small changes in the characteristic being measured.

Variability or Precision:

- The *repeatability* is the ability of the measurement system to return the same measured value when one operator takes repeated measurements of the same unit.

- The *reproducibility* is the degree of agreement when multiple operators measure the same characteristic on the same unit.

Attribute Data

For attribute data, the measurement system is comprised of the units being measured, the gauge, and the operators and their methods. In this MSA, the operators are frequently the gauge and the evaluation consists of how well they can look at a characteristic to either determine its acceptability (yes/no) or properly rate it on a scale. Examples include operators inspecting rolls of cloth for defects, or an operator's ability to complete a purchase order form properly. This type of MSA can determine whether:

1. An operator can repeat his or her measures when evaluating many units multiple times (*within operator* variation).

2. An operator cannot only repeat his or her own measures on multiple units, but can match those measures to known standards for the units (accuracy).

3. Multiple operators can match the measurements of one another on multiple units (*between operator* variation).

4. Multiple operators not only match the measurements of one another on multiple units, but can all match the known standard for these units.

How do I do it? 🏃

MSA for Variable Data

A. **Bias** - To determine whether bias exists in the system:

1. Obtain a known standard that represents a value within the normal range of the characteristic of interest.

2. Have one operator with one gauge measure the known standard a minimum of ten times, record these values, and calculate the average.

3. Compare the average to the known standard.

- If the average is less than the known standard, then offset the gauge positively by this amount.

- If the average is greater than the known standard, then offset the gauge negatively by this amount.

Example:

A known standard was obtained and certified to be 0.500". One operator using one gauge measured this standard ten times and determined the average value to be 0.496". Because the average value is 0.004" less than the standard, the gauge must be positively offset by 0.004".

 ©2002 GOAL/QPC, Six Sigma Academy

Bias

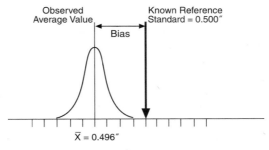

$\overline{X} = 0.496''$

B. **Linearity - To determine whether bias exists over the operating range of the gauge:**

1. Identify four or more standard/reference units that span the likely range over which the measurement system is to be used.

2. Identify one operator to determine the bias of the gauge over the operating range of the process variation.

3. Create a scatter plot with the standard/ reference units on the x axis and the bias values on the y axis.

4. Create a regression equation for this data and determine whether the goodness of fit term (R^2) is acceptable.

- The slope of the regression line determines the linearity. Generally, the lower the absolute value of the slope, the better the linearity; the converse is also true (the higher the absolute value of the slope, the worse the linearity).

Example:

A linearity study was conducted in which six samples that spanned the operating range of the gauge were identified and certified. (Certified is when a unit is measured with a known high precision instrument.) One operator measured each of the six samples ten times and the bias for the six units was calculated. The data was graphed using a fitted line plot and the fit was assessed using R^2.

Linearity

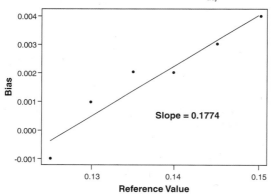

Regression Plot

Bias = -0.0225238 + 0.177143 Reference Value
S = 0.0005255 R^2 = 92.6% R^2_{adj} = 90.7%

Slope = 0.1774

If the system is determined to be nonlinear, check for a defective gauge, wrong standard/reference values, incorrect operator methods of measuring, or an improperly calibrated gauge.

C. **Stability - To determine whether the measurement system's bias is drifting over time:**

1. Obtain a standard/reference unit that falls in the mid-range of the production values.
2. On a regular basis (weekly or monthly), measure the standard/reference value three to five times.

3. Plot this data in X-bar ($\overline{X}$) and R control charts.

4. Monitor these charts regularly to determine whether the gauge needs to be calibrated.

5. If desired, create the same control charts for reference values on the low and high side of production.

Example:

A standard/reference value is measured three times on a weekly basis. The data is plotted in an $\overline{X}$ and R control chart.

Stability

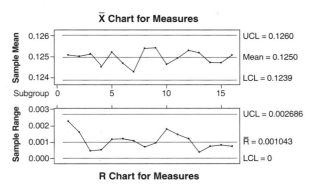

$\overline{X}$ Chart for Measures

R Chart for Measures

Both charts are used to determine the stability or repeatability of the measurements over time. The R chart captures the *within subgroup* (multiple readings of the same part) variation over time. The R chart generates the control limits for the $\overline{X}$ chart. Captured *between subgroups* (as shown in the $\overline{X}$ chart) are the week-to-week average measures of the test part. Because the $\overline{X}$ chart is in control, the measurement system is exhibiting good stability over time. If there was an issue with stability, a design of experiments could be applied to determine the contributors to the poor stability.

Discrimination

Discrimination is the ability of the measurement system to detect small changes in the characteristic of interest. As a general rule, the measurement system should be able to discriminate to one-tenth the tolerance (USL - LSL).

Example:

If a critical characteristic of a part is its length, and the lower and upper specification limits are 1.500" and 1.550", respectively, the measurement system should be able to measure to one-tenth the tolerance or (1.550" - 1.500")/10 = 0.005". Therefore, at a minimum, any gauge used needs to measure to 0.005".

Discrimination

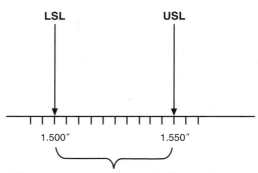

The measurement system must be able to resolve the tolerance to ten equal divisions of 0.005".

Consider instead in this example, if the measurement system could only measure to 0.050". In this case, these parts could only be classified as meeting the upper or lower specification limit and nothing in between. Therefore, this gauge would not provide adequate discrimination to properly accept or reject parts.

MSA Components of Variation

Any measurement of a part not only measures the true part value, but also measures any variability that may exist because of the poor repeatability of the gauge and/or the poor reproducibility of the operators and their methods of measuring. Obviously, it is desirable to ascertain the true part value free of any other source of variability to determine the true capability of the process. A test known as a Gauge Repeatability & Reproducibility (GR&R) test is conducted to determine whether excessive variability exists in the measurement system. This test is designed such that the sources of variability within the measurement system, which include the total variability (TV), the product variability, and the measurement system variability (also known as measurement system error or precision, P), can be partitioned as shown in the following figure:

MSA Components of Variation

$$\hat{\sigma}^2 \; Total \;\; = \;\; \hat{\sigma}^2 \; product \;\; + \;\; \hat{\sigma}^2 \; ms$$

Total variability = product variability + measurement system variability

$$\hat{\sigma}^2 \; repeatability \;\; + \;\; \hat{\sigma}^2 \; reproducibility$$

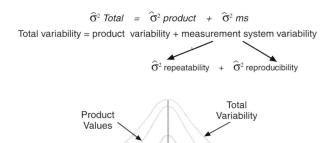

As shown in the figure, measurement system variability can further be partitioned into:

- Measurement system repeatability: The ability of one operator using one gauge to measure one part multiple times with minimal variability.

- Measurement system reproducibility: The ability of multiple operators to produce similar average measures for multiple parts, with minimal variability in the average measured values.

Once all of these variances have been calculated, the organization can determine whether the measurement system is reliable based on the following calculations. If the measurement system is deemed unreliable, these variances can help determine whether the problem is repeatability and/or reproducibility.

GR&R Acceptance Criteria

	% Contribution	% P/TV	% P/T
	$\dfrac{\hat{\sigma}^2\,ms}{\hat{\sigma}^2\,Total}\times 100$	$\dfrac{\hat{\sigma}\,ms}{\hat{\sigma}\,Total}\times 100$	$\dfrac{5.15\times\hat{\sigma}ms}{Tolerance}\times 100$
Marginally Acceptable	<9%	<30%	<30%
Good	<4%	<20%	<20%
Excellent	<1%	<10%	<10%

- *Percent Contribution* is the preferred Six Sigma metric. It is similar to the P/TV ratio described below, but it is a ratio of variances. Recall from basic statistics that variances add; the Percent Contribution for each source of variation will sum to 100%, making it easier to identify the greatest source of variation.

- *Precision to Total Variation* (P/TV) is the ratio of the measurement system standard deviation to the total

©2002 GOAL/QPC, Six Sigma Academy

observed standard deviation. This metric is used to determine if the organization can measure its process variation well enough to validate its process improvements through hypothesis testing.

The total variation can be estimated in two ways: 1) It may be estimated using a historical standard deviation of the process. 2) If the samples from the study represent the process distribution, the standard deviation of the study may be used as an estimate of the process.

• *Precision to Tolerance* (P / T) is the ratio of 5.15 times the measurement system standard deviation, to the tolerance (USL - LSL). This metric is used to determine if the organization can appropriately accept or reject product. (The value "5.15" is the number of standard deviations needed to capture 99% of the variation.) The P / T ratio is often a requirement of the quality system, especially in the automotive industry. Caution should be taken to ensure that the tolerancing on the product is realistic. Inflated tolerances can make a measurement system "look" better than it actually is.

How do I do a Continuous GR&R test?

1. Identify the characteristic on the unit to be measured, the gauge, and the operators who use the gauge.

2. Identify a number of units (typically ten units) that span the range of the long-term process variability.

   • This may require samples to be collected over several days or weeks.

3. Conduct the GR&R in the environment where the measurement takes place.

4. Estimate repeatability and reproducibility by conducting a test using three operators and ten

units. The units need to be measured at least twice by each operator.

- This test should be randomized; therefore, have the first operator measure the ten units in random order, then have the second operator measure the ten units in random order, and then the third operator. After the operators have measured all of the units once, they are to measure the units again in random order to obtain the repeat measures. There should be a total of sixty measures in this designed test (3 x 10 x 2).

5. **Calculate the variances using the ANOVA method.**

- Many software packages can be used to calculate variances using the ANOVA method.

6. **Interpret the results graphically and analytically to determine whether the measurement system is acceptable, needs repair, or must be replaced.**

Example:

A Black Belt needed to determine the baseline capability of the filament diameter of a light bulb. However, prior to determining capability, the Black Belt knew she had to conduct an MSA. She selected ten filaments, the gauge used to measure these filaments, and three operators to use this gauge. She then created the following sampling plan:

MSA Sampling Plan

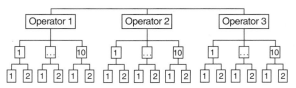

- Three operators, ten parts, two trial measures
- Each operator measures the same ten parts, twice in random order.

The following figure shows what the graphical output of this MSA would look like.

MSA Graphical Results

Gauge R&R (ANOVA) for Measure

Gauge name: Baseline MSA
Date of study: 11-15-01
Reported by: VLK
Tolerance: 1.5
Misc:

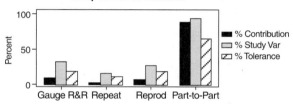

Components of Variation

■ % Contribution
☐ % Study Var
▨ % Tolerance

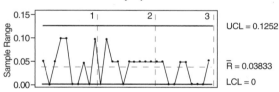

R Chart by Operator

UCL = 0.1252
$\bar{R}$ = 0.03833
LCL = 0

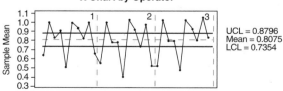

X̄ Chart by Operator

UCL = 0.8796
Mean = 0.8075
LCL = 0.7354

Continued on next page

MSA Graphical Results, continued

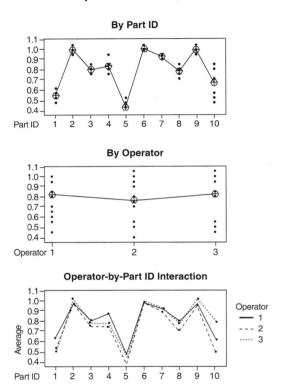

By Part ID

By Operator

Operator-by-Part ID Interaction

Interpreting the graphical results:

When interpreting the results, it is important to always assess the range chart (R chart) for stability first. Assessing the range chart for stability ensures that there are no special causes. (Special causes should be corrected and the MSA repeated.) Special causes in the range chart will increase the average range and in turn will inflate the distance between the control limits in the average chart. In the filament example above, the range chart is in control; therefore, the system is stable.

Secondly, it is important to assess discrimination from the range chart. A recommended guideline is to ensure that at least five levels of possible values in the range chart, including zero, are evident. A lack of discrimination may also be the result of rounding-off values. There are only three levels of values, including zero, in our example. This is an immediate flag that discrimination of the gauge being used to measure the filaments may be an issue, unless the inspectors are rounding the measures.

Captured in the range chart are measures within part. This variation is reflected between the control limits on the average ($\overline{X}$) chart. Captured in the average chart is the part-to-part variation between operators. In our example, fifty to seventy percent of the averages are outside of the control limits on the average chart, indicating that the variation *within subgroup* (measurement within part) is less than the variation *between subgroup* (part-to-part). Ideally, we want to be able to detect part-to-part variation, so out-of-control points on the average chart are desired in this case. Measurement variation should be much less than part-to-part variation, as indicated in this example.

Software packages offer charts other than just the $\overline{X}$ and R charts. The components of variation bar chart in this MINITAB™ software output indicates that the largest source of variation is part-to-part. Repeatability is small compared to reproducibility. The total Gauge R&R (% contribution) is the sum of the variance components of reproducibility and repeatability compared to the total study variance.

Reproducibility is evidenced in the average chart between operators 1, 2, and 3. The "By Operator" chart is an overlay of the patterns in the average chart for each operator. Because the operators measured the same parts, the same results or patterns from part-to-part would be expected between operators.

Because the sampling plan is "crossed" (see the Multi-Vari charts chapter in this book for more information on crossed designs) between operator and part, there is a potential for an operator-by-part interaction. This is indicated by the crossing lines in the "Operator-by-Part ID Interaction" chart, which shows that not all operators measure the same parts the same way.

Interpreting the analytical results:

The following figure shows the MSA analytical results for the filament example previously cited.

MSA Analytical Results

Source	% StdDev (SD)	% Study Var (5.15 x SD)	% Study Var (%SV)	Tolerance (SV/T)	Contribution (of VarComp)
Total Gauge R&R	0.066615	0.34306	32.66	22.87	10.67
Repeatability	0.035940	0.18509	17.62	12.34	3.10
Reproducibility	0.056088	0.28885	27.50	19.26	7.56
Operator	0.030200	0.15553	14.81	10.37	2.19
Operator-by-Part ID	0.047263	0.24340	23.17	16.23	5.37
Part-To-Part	0.192781	0.99282	94.52	66.19	89.33
Total Variation	0.203965	1.05042	100.00	70.03	100.00

According to these results, the measurement system is unacceptable because the measurement system variation (total GR&R) of 10.67% is too high. Values less than 9% are acceptable and less than 1% is considered excellent. (See the GR&R Acceptance Criteria table earlier in this chapter.)

It appears the majority of the variation in the measurement system (10.67%) is due to reproducibility (7.56%). Therefore, the organization's goal is to determine why the measurements are not reproducible. Reproducibility is broken down into its components of operator and operator-by-part interaction. The interaction accounts for 5.37% of the total process variation. The question the organization would have to answer to solve this problem is why some operators measure some parts differently than others.

Destructive Testing

In many instances, the characteristic being measured (i.e., strength or moisture) is destroyed during the measurement, so a second or third operator cannot measure the same part.

Typically, a GR&R uses *ten* parts, three operators, and two measures per part for a total of sixty measures. To conduct the GR&R where the parts are destroyed, ten batches with six parts per batch are needed, for a total of *sixty* parts that are measured. The batches must be produced such that they represent the long-term variability of the process and the parts contained within a batch are assumed to be consistent.

Each operator will measure two parts per batch and the results will be analyzed. This destructive GR&R uses a nested ANOVA to analyze the data vs. a crossed ANOVA in the nondestructive test. (Nested refers to parts being unique to the operator.)

MSA for Attribute Data

When the characteristic to be measured is attribute in nature (e.g., the correct name in a field on a form, the correct color blue, or a rank on a scale by an operator), then the organization would need to conduct an

Attribute Gauge Repeatability & Reproducibility study. Depending on the test, the objective of the study would be to ensure operators can either discern between good and bad or rank a characteristic on a scale and get the correct answer. In this test, the operator is frequently the gauge.

How do I do an Attribute GR&R study?

1. **Identify thirty to 100 items to be evaluated.**

   • Typically more samples are needed in an attribute study because of the nature of data.

2. **Have a person who has knowledge of the customer requirements for this characteristic rate these items on the scale that is used in daily operations.**

   • Record their responses for all thirty to 100 items in a column of data called "attribute" or "reference standard."

3. **Identify the people who need to measure the items.**

4. **Have the first person rate all thirty to 100 items in random order and record these values.**

   • Repeat this step for each subsequent person, recording this data.

5. **Repeat step four such that each operator has a chance at a repeat measure and record this data.**

Several important measures from this test are identified in the following example.

Attribute GR&R Measures

Known Population		Operator #1		Operator #2		Operator #3	
Sample	Attribute	Try #1	Try #2	Try #1	Try #2	Try #1	Try #2
1	pass ②	pass	pass	pass ① pass		fail	fail
2	pass	pass	pass	pass	pass	fail	fail
3	fail	fail	fail	fail ③ pass		fail	fail
4	fail	fail	fail	fail	fail	fail	fail
5	fail	fail	fail	pass	fail	fail	fail
6	pass	pass	pass ④	pass	pass	pass	pass

1. The number of times an operator can repeat the measured value. If an operator measured thirty items twice and successfully repeated the measures twenty-six times, then he or she had an 86.6% success rate. Each operator will have a success rate for their repeat measures.

2. The number of times an operator not only repeats the measures, but these repeats match the known standard. Although an operator may have successfully repeated their measures 86.6% of the time, the measure may have only matched the known standard twenty-three times out of thirty, for a 76.6% success rate. This implies that an operator may not understand the criteria for the known standard.

3. The number of times all of the operators match their repeat measures. If three operators evaluate thirty parts and all of the operators match their repeats twenty-two times, then this is a 73.3% success rate.

4. The number of times all of the operators match their repeat measures and all these measures match the known standards. If three operators match all of these measures twenty times out of thirty, then this is a success rate of 66.6%.

This last measure is the measure used to determine the effectiveness of the measurement system. In general, it should be greater than 80% (preferably 90%), assuming that the study was done with three operators and two trials. If the value is less than 80%, then opportunities for improvement need to be identified. Typically, the solution is either training of the operators, better definition of the known standard, or an improvement to the environment in the area where the item is being measured.

Example:

When a customer places an order, a system operator is responsible for finding information in a database and then transferring that information to the order form. Recently, customers have been receiving the wrong product, and the data suggests that the problem may be in transferring this information. For the Black Belt to determine the capability of this process, an Attribute GR&R must first be conducted. To do this, the Black Belt creates thirty different fake orders, with known correct answers. Next the operators are asked to find the required information in the database to determine whether the operators can get the correct answer or not. The answers to this test are included in the following chart.

Attribute GR&R Effectiveness

Known Population		Operator #1		Operator #2		Operator #3		Agree *	Agree **
Sample #	Attribute	Try #1	Try #2	Try #1	Try #2	Try #1	Try #2	Y/N	Y/N
1	Pass	Pass	Pass	Pass	Pass	Pass	Pass	Y	Y
2	Pass	Pass	Pass	Pass	Pass	Pass	Pass	Y	Y
3	Pass	Pass	Pass	Pass	Pass	Pass	Pass	Y	Y
4	Pass	Pass	Pass	Pass	Pass	Fail	Pass	Y	Y
5	Fail	Fail	Fail	Fail	Fail	Pass	Fail	N	N
6	Fail	Pass	Pass	Pass	Pass	Pass	Pass	N	N
7	Pass	Pass	Pass	Pass	Pass	Pass	Pass	Y	N
8	Fail	Fail	Fail	Fail	Fail	Fail	Fail	Y	Y
27	Pass	Pass	Pass	Pass	Pass	Pass	Fail	Y	
28	Fail	Fail	Fail	Fail	Fail	Fail	Fail	Y	Y
29	Pass	Pass	Pass	Pass	Pass	Pass	Pass	Y	Y
30	Pass	Pass	Pass	Pass	Pass	Pass	Pass		
	% Appraiser Score		100.00%		100.00%		83.33%		
	%Score vs. Attribute		93.33%		96.67%		80.00%		
						Screen % Effective Score		80.00%	
						Screen % Effective Score vs. Attribute			76.67%

* All operators agree with themselves and each other.

** All operators agree with themselves and each other, and with the standard.

Note:
• The target for all scores is 100%. Less than 80% is a reasonable lower limit for most cases.
• The % Appraiser Score is the repeatability and shows when the operator agrees with himself/herself on both trials.
• The % Score vs. Attribute is a score of the individual error against a known population and shows when the operator agrees on both trials with the known standard.
• The Screen % Effective score shows when all operators agreed within and between themselves.
• The Screen % Effective vs. Attribute is the total error against a known population and shows when all operators agreed with and between themselves and agreed with the known standard.

According to these results, the measurement system is unacceptable because the screen % effective score vs. attribute is less than 80%.

Capability Indices

Why use it?

Process capability refers to the capability of a process to consistently make a product that meets a customer-specified specification range (tolerance). Capability indices are used to predict the performance of a process by comparing the width of process variation to the width of the specified tolerance. It is used extensively in many industries and only has meaning if the process being studied is stable (in statistical control).

What does it do?

Capability indices allow calculations for both short-term (C_p and C_{pk}) and/or long-term (P_p and P_{pk}) performance for a process whose output is measured using variable data at a specific opportunity for a defect.

Short-Term Capability Indices

The short-term capability indices C_p and C_{pk} are measures calculated using the short-term process standard deviation. Because the short-term process variation is used, these measures are free of subgroup drift in the data and take into account only the *within subgroup* variation.

C_p is a ratio of the customer-specified tolerance to six standard deviations of the short-term process variation. C_p is calculated without regard to location of the data mean within the tolerance, so it gives an indication of what the process could perform to if the mean of the data was centered between the specification limits. Because of this assumption, C_p is sometimes referred to as the process potential.

C_{pk} is a ratio of the distance between the process average and the closest specification limit, to three standard deviations of the short-term process variation. Because C_{pk} takes into account location of the data mean within the tolerance, it is a more realistic measure of the process capability. C_{pk} is sometimes referred to as the process performance.

Long-Term Capability Indices

The long-term capability indices P_p and P_{pk} are measures calculated using the long-term process standard deviation. Because the long-term process variation is used, these measures take into account subgroup drift in the data as well as the *within subgroup* variation.

P_p is a ratio of the customer-specified tolerance to six standard deviations of the long-term process variation. Like C_p, P_p is calculated without regard to location of the data mean within the tolerance.

P_{pk} is a ratio of the distance between the process average and the closest specification limit, to three standard deviations of the long-term process variation. Like C_{pk}, P_{pk} takes into account the location of the data mean within the tolerance. Because P_{pk} uses the long-term variation in the process and takes into account the process centering within the specified tolerance, it is a good indicator of the process performance the customer is seeing.

What is a good C_p/C_{pk} or P_p/P_{pk} value?

Because both C_p and C_{pk} are ratios of the tolerance width to the process variation, larger values of C_p and C_{pk} are better. The larger the C_p and C_{pk}, the wider the tolerance width relative to the process variation. The same is also true for P_p and P_{pk}.

What determines a "good" value depends on the definition of "good." A C_p of 1.33 is approximately equivalent to a short-term Z of 4. A P_{pk} of 1.33 is approximately equivalent to a long-term Z of 4. However, a Six Sigma process typically has a short-term Z of 6 or a long-term Z of 4.5.

How do I do it?

The type of data available (short-term or long-term) will determine whether C_p / C_{pk} or P_p / P_{pk} can be calculated. The following mathematical formulas are used to calculate these indices.

$$C_p = (USL - LSL)/6\sigma_{st}$$

Where σ_{st} = short-term pooled standard deviation.

$$P_p = (USL - LSL)/6\sigma_{lt}$$

Where σ_{lt} = long-term standard deviation.

Capability Indices

Short-term Capability Indices

$$C_p = \frac{USL - LSL}{6\,\sigma_{st}}$$

$$C_{pk} = \min(C_{pk(USL)}, C_{pk\,(LSL)})$$

$$C_{pk(USL)} = \frac{(USL - \bar{X})}{3\,\sigma_{st}}$$

$$C_{pk(LSL)} = \frac{(\bar{X} - LSL)}{3\,\sigma_{st}}$$

Long-term Capability Indices

$$P_p = \frac{USL - LSL}{6\,\sigma_{lt}}$$

$$P_{pk} = \min(P_{pk(USL)}, P_{pk\,(LSL)})$$

$$P_{pk(USL)} = \frac{(USL - \bar{X})}{3\,\sigma_{lt}}$$

$$P_{pk(LSL)} = \frac{(\bar{X} - LSL)}{3\,\sigma_{lt}}$$

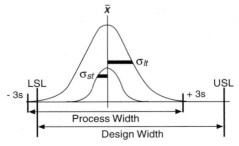

Manufacturing Example:

Suppose the diameter of a spark plug is a critical dimension that needs to conform to lower and upper customer specification limits of 0.480" and 0.490", respectively. Five randomly selected spark plugs are measured in every work shift. Each of the five samples on each work shift is called a subgroup. Subgroups have been collected for three months on a stable process. The average of all the data was 0.487". The short-term standard deviation has been calculated and was determined to be 0.0013". The long-term standard deviation was determined to be 0.019".

To Calculate C_p and C_{pk}:

C_p = (0.490" - 0.480")/(6 x 0.0013) = 0.010/0.0078 = 1.28

C_{pl} = (0.487 - 0.480)/(3 x 0.0013) = 0.007/0.0039 = 1.79

C_{pu} = (0.490 - 0.487)/(3 x 0.0013) = 0.003/0.0039 = 0.77

$$C_{pk} = min (C_{pl}, C_{pu})$$

$$C_{pk} = min (1.79, 0.77) = 0.77$$

To Calculate P_p and P_{pk}:

P_p = (0.490" - 0.480")/(6 x 0.019) = 0.0100/0.114 = 0.09

P_{pl} = (0.487 - 0.480)/(3 x 0.019) = 0.007/0.057 = 0.12

P_{pu} = (0.490 - 0.487)/(3 x 0.019) = 0.003/0.057 = 0.05

$$P_{pk} = min (P_{pl}, P_{pu})$$

$$P_{pk} = min (0.12, 0.05) = 0.05$$

In this example, C_p is 1.28. Because C_p is the ratio of the specified tolerance to the process variation, a C_p value of 1.28 indicates that the process is capable of delivering product that meets the specified tolerance (if the process is centered). (A C_p greater than 1 indicates the process can deliver a product that meets the specifications at least 99.73% of the time.) Any improvements to the process to increase our value of 1.28 would require a reduction in the variability within our subgroups. C_p, however, is calculated without regard to the process centering within the specified tolerance. A centered process is rarely the case so a C_{pk} value must be calculated.

C_{pk} considers the location of the process data average. In this calculation, we are comparing the average of our process to the closest specification limit and dividing by three short-term standard deviations. In our example, C_{pk} is 0.77. In contrast to the C_p measurement, the C_{pk} measurement clearly shows that the process is incapable of producing product that meets the specified tolerance. Any improvements to our process to increase our value of 0.77 would require a mean shift in the data towards the center of the tolerance and/or a reduction in the *within subgroup* variation. (**Note**: For centered processes, C_p and C_{pk} will be the same.)

Our P_p is 0.09. Because P_p is the ratio of the specified tolerance to the process variation, a P_p value of 0.09 indicates that the process is incapable of delivering product that meets the specified tolerance. Any improvements to the process to increase our value of 0.09 would require a reduction in the variability within and/or between subgroups. P_p, however, is calculated without regard to the process centering within the specified tolerance. A centered process is rarely the case so a P_{pk} value, which accounts for lack of process centering, will surely indicate poor capability for our process as well. (**Note**: For both P_p and C_p, we assume no drifting of the subgroup averages.)

P_{pk} represents the actual long-term performance of the process and is the index that most likely represents what customers receive. In the example, P_{pk} is 0.05, confirming our P_p result of poor process performance. Any improvements to the process to increase our value of 0.05 would require a mean shift in the data towards the center of the tolerance and/or a reduction in the *within subgroup* and *between subgroup* variations.

Business Process Example:

Suppose a call center reports to its customers that it will resolve their issue within fifteen minutes. This fifteen-minute time limit is the upper specification limit. It is desirable to resolve the issue as soon as possible; therefore, there is no lower specification limit. The call center operates twenty-four hours a day in eight-hour shifts. Six calls are randomly measured every shift and recorded for two months. An SPC chart shows the process is stable. The average of the data is 11.7 minutes, the short-term pooled standard deviation is 1.2 minutes, and the long-term standard deviation is 2.8 minutes.

To Calculate C_p and C_{pk}:

C_p = cannot be calculated as there is no LSL

C_{pl} = undefined

$C_{pu} = (15 - 11.7)/(3 \times 1.2) = 3.3/3.6 = 0.92$

$C_{pk} = min (C_{pl}, C_{pu}) = 0.92$

To Calculate P_p and P_{pk}:

P_p = cannot be calculated as there is no LSL

P_{pl} = undefined

$P_{pu} = (15 - 11.7)/(3 \times 2.8) = 3.3/8.4 = 0.39$

$P_{pk} = min (P_{pl}, P_{pu}) = 0.39$

In this example, we can only evaluate C_{pk} and P_{pk} as there is no lower limit. These numbers indicate that if we can eliminate *between subgroup* variation, we could achieve a process capability (P_{pk}) of 0.92, which is our current C_{pk}.

 **Graphical Analysis**

Why use it?

Graphical analysis is an effective way to present data.

What does it do?

Graphs allow an organization to represent data (either variable or attribute) to evaluate central tendency and spread, detect patterns in the data, and identify sources of variation in the process.

How do I do it?

The type of data collected will determine the type of graph used to represent the data. Described below are some common graphs for different data types.

Histograms

Histograms are an efficient graphical method for describing the distribution of data. However, a large enough sample (greater than fifty data points) is required to effectively show the distribution. Data is divided into groups called "classes." The number of data points within a class is counted and bars are drawn for each class. The shape of the resultant histogram can be used to assess:

- Measures of central tendency,
- Variation in the data,
- Shape or underlying distribution of the data (when compared to a normal distribution).

A Histogram

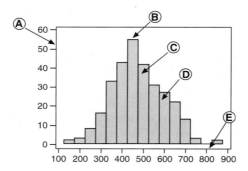

A. The vertical axis shows the frequency or percentage of data points in each class.

B. The modal class is the class with the highest frequency.

C. The frequency is the number of data points found in each class.

D. Each bar is one class or interval.

E. The horizontal axis shows the scale of measure for the Critical To characteristics.

Software packages are available that will automatically calculate the class intervals and allow the user to revise them as required. The number of intervals shown can influence the pattern of the sample.

Plotting the data is always recommended. Three unique distributions of data are shown on the following page. All three data plots share an identical mean, but the spread of the data about the mean differs significantly.

> *Tip* Always look for twin or multiple peaks indicating that the data comes from two or more sources (e.g., machines, shifts, people, suppliers). If multiple peaks are evident, the data must then be stratified.

Three Distributions of Data

Normal

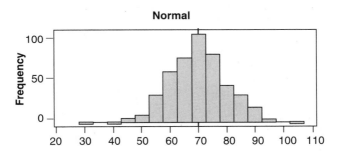

Negative Skew

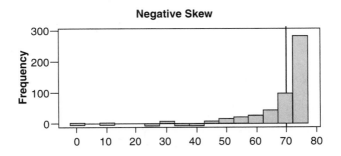

Positive Skew

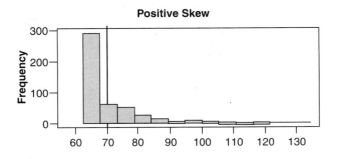

The following histogram illustrates a distribution where the measures of central tendency (mean, median, and mode) are equal.

Symmetric Data

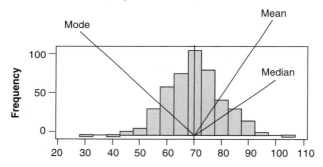

This is a normal distribution, sometimes referred to as a bell-shaped curve. Notice that there is a single point of central tendency and the data are symmetrically distributed about the center.

Some processes are naturally skewed. A negatively skewed distribution is shown in the following figure:

Negatively Skewed Data

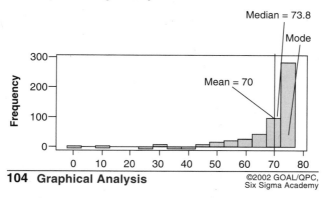

For skewed-left data, the median is between the mode and mean, with the mean on the left. This distribution does not appear normally distributed and may require transformation prior to statistical analysis. Data that sometimes exhibit negative skewness are cash flow, yield, and strength.

A positively skewed distribution is shown in the following figure:

Positively Skewed Data

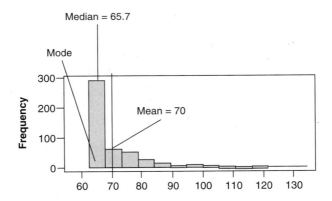

The long tail of the skewed distribution points in the positive x-direction. The median is between the mode and the mean, with the mean on the right. This distribution is not normally distributed and is another candidate for transformation. Data that sometimes exhibit positive skewness are home prices, salaries, cycle time of delivery, and surface roughness.

(For more information on histograms, refer to *The Memory Jogger*™*II*.)

Box and Whisker Plot

A box and whisker plot can be used to view variability and centering, based on quartiles, in a variable output (y) vs. an attribute input (x) at one or more levels.

Box & Whisker Plot

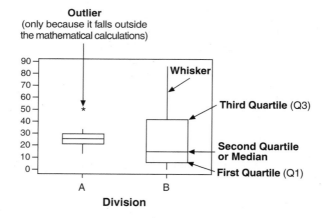

- *Quartiles* rank-order the data and identify the twenty-fifth, fiftieth, and seventy-fifth percentile.

- The *Interquartile (IQ) Range* is equal to the range between the first and third quartile (Q3 - Q1).

- *Whiskers* are limited by a mathematical calculation. The upper whisker cannot be longer than Q3 + 1.5 x (Q3 - Q1). The whisker line is drawn to the largest value in the data set *below* this calculated value. If there are data points above this value, they show up as asterisks to indicate they may be outliers. The same is true for the lower whisker with a limit of Q1 - 1.5 x (Q3 - Q1). The whisker line is then drawn to the smallest value in the data set *above* this calculated value.

Dot Plot

The dot plot shows variability in a sample of variable or attribute data. Multiple dot plots can be constructed for discrete levels of another variable.

Dot Plot

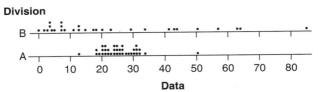

Multiple occurrences are stacked vertically along the x axis. Notice how the discrete levels for Divisions A and B lay above one another, making the dot plot an effective tool for comparing central location and variability within and between divisions.

Scatter Diagram

The scatter diagram is used to determine whether a qualitative relationship, linear or curvilinear, exists between two continuous or discrete variables. Scatter diagrams provide verification of a Cause & Effect Diagram or Matrix to determine if there is more than just a consensus connection between causes and effects.

The scatter diagram on the following page shows a strong positive relationship between the number of customers and the number of suppliers; as the number of customers increases, so does the number of suppliers.

Scatter Diagram

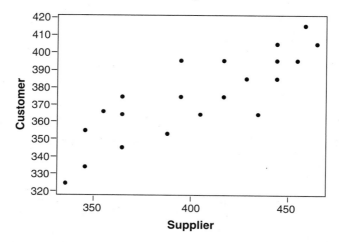

Subsequent analysis such as correlation and regression are typically used to quantify the relationship in a scatter diagram.

> **Tip** The scatter diagram does not predict cause and effect relationships; it only shows the strength of the relationship between two variables. The stronger the relationship, the greater the likelihood that change in one variable will affect change in another variable.

(For more information on scatter diagrams, refer to *The Memory Jogger™II*.)

Run Chart

Why use it?

Run Charts allow a team to study observed data (a performance measure of a process) for trends or patterns over a specified period of time.

What does it do?

A Run Chart:

- Monitors the performance of one or more processes over time to detect trends, shifts, or cycles.

- Allows a team to compare a performance measure before and after implementation of a solution, to measure its impact.

- Focuses attention on truly vital changes in the process.

- Tracks useful information for predicting trends.

How do I do it?

1. **Decide on the process performance measure.**

2. **Gather data.**

   - Generally, 20-25 data points should be collected to detect meaningful patterns.

3. **Create a graph with a vertical line (y axis) and a horizontal line (x axis).**

   - On the vertical line (y axis), draw the scale related to the variable being measured.

     - Arrange the y axis to cover the full range of the measurements and then some (e.g., $1\frac{1}{2}$ times the range of data).

   - On the horizontal line (x axis), draw the time or sequence scale.

4. **Plot the data.**

   • Look at the data collected. If there are no obvious trends, calculate the average or arithmetic mean. The average is the sum of the measured values divided by the number of data points. (The median value can also be used but the mean is the most frequently used measure of the "centering" of the sample.) Draw a horizontal line at the average value.

   Tip Do not redraw this average line every time new data is added. Only when there has been a significant change in the process or prevailing conditions should the average be recalculated and redrawn, and then only using the data points after the verified change.

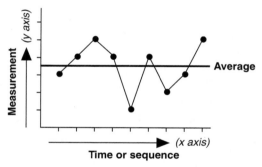

5. **Interpret the chart.**

   • Note the position of the average line. Is it where it should be relative to a customer need or specification? Is it where the organization wants it to be, relative to the business objective?

   Tip A danger in using a Run Chart is the tendency to see every variation in data as being important. The Run Chart should be used to focus on truly vital changes in the process. Simple tests can be used to look for meaningful trends and patterns. (These tests are found in the "Determining if the Process is Out of Control" section of the Control Charts chapter of this book. Remember that for more sophisticated uses, a Control Chart is invaluable because it is simply a Run Chart with statistically based limits.)

**Average Number of Days
for Determining Eligibility for Services**

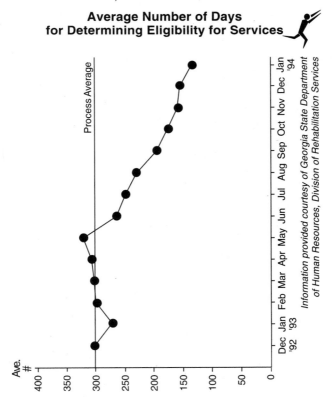

Information provided courtesy of Georgia State Department of Human Resources, Division of Rehabilitation Services

Note: Eligibility requirements changed in May, making it much simpler for the department staff to make determinations. The trend is statistically significant because there are six or more consecutive points declining.

Pareto Chart

Why use it?

A Pareto Chart focuses efforts on the problems that offer the greatest potential for improvement by showing their relative frequency or size in a descending bar graph.

What does it do?

A Pareto Chart:

- Helps a team focus on those causes that will have the greatest impact if solved.

- Is based on the proven Pareto principle: 20% of the sources cause 80% of any problem.

- Displays the relative importance of problems in a simple, quickly interpreted, visual format.

- Helps prevent "shifting the problem" where the "solution" removes some causes but worsens others.

- Measures progress in a highly visible format that provides incentive to push on for more improvement.

How do I do it?

1. Decide which problem to focus on.

2. Using brainstorming or existing data, choose the causes or problems that will be monitored, compared, and rank-ordered.

   - A brainstorming session may ask "What are typical problems that users ask about a telephone help line?" Questions based on existing data may ask, "What problems in the last month have users called in to the help line?"

3. **Choose the most meaningful unit of measurement such as frequency or cost.**

   • Sometimes it is difficult to know before the study is done which unit of measurement is best. Be prepared to do both frequency and cost.

4. **Choose the time period for the study.**

   • Choose a time period that is long enough to represent the situation. Longer studies don't always translate to better information. Look first at volume and variety within the data.

   • Make sure the scheduled time is typical in order to take into account seasonality or even different patterns within a given day or week.

5. **Gather the necessary data on each problem category either by "real time" or reviewing historical data.**

   • Whether data is gathered in real time or historically, Check Sheets are the easiest method for collecting data.

   Tip *Always* include with the source data and the final chart, the identifiers that indicate the source, location, and time period covered.

6. **Compare the relative frequency or cost of each problem category.**

7. **List the problem categories on a horizontal line and frequencies on a vertical line.**

   • List the categories in descending order from left to right on the horizontal line with bars above each problem category to indicate its frequency or cost. List the unit of measure on the vertical line.

8. **(Optional) Draw the cumulative percentage line showing the portion of the total that each problem category represents.**

   a) On the vertical line (opposite the raw data, #, $, etc.), record 100% opposite the total number and 50% at the halfway point. Fill in the remaining percentages drawn to scale.

b) Starting with the highest problem category, draw a dot or mark an x at the upper righthand corner of the bar.

- Add the total of the next problem category to the first and draw a dot above that bar showing both the cumulative number and percentage. Connect the dots and record the remaining cumulative totals until 100% is reached.

9. Interpret the results.

- Generally, the tallest bars indicate the biggest contributors to the overall problem. Dealing with these problem categories first therefore makes common sense. *But the most frequent or expensive is not always the most important.* Always ask, What has the most impact on the goals of our business and customers?

Example:

Consider the case of HOTrep, an internal computer network help line. The parent organization wanted to know what problems the people calling in to the HOTrep help line were experiencing. A team was created to brainstorm possible problems to monitor for comparison. They choose frequency as the most important measure because the project team could use this information to simplify software, improve documentation or training, or solve bigger system problems. HOTrep help line calls were reviewed for ten weeks and data from these calls was gathered based on a review of incident reports (historical data).

Problem Category	Frequency	Percent (%)
Bad configuration	3	1
Boot problems	68	33
File problems	8	4
Lat. connection	20	10
Print problems	16	8
Reflection hang	24	12
Reflection sys. integrity	11	5
Reflections misc.	6	3
System configuration	16	8
System integrity	19	9
Others	15	7
Total	**206**	

The data was displayed in a Pareto Chart and helped the team determine that it should focus on "Boot problems," to have the greatest impact on its customers.

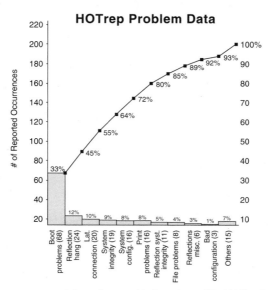

Information provided courtesy of SmithKline Beecham

Variations

The Pareto Chart is one of the most widely and creatively used improvement tools. The variations used most frequently are:

A. *Major Cause Breakdowns* in which the "tallest bar" is broken into subcauses in a second, linked Pareto.

B. *Before and After* in which the "new Pareto" bars are drawn side by side with the original Pareto, showing the effect of a change. It can be drawn as one chart or two separate charts.

C. *Change the Source of Data* in which data is collected on the same problem but from different departments, locations, equipment, and so on, and shown in side-by-side Pareto Charts.

D. *Change Measurement Scale* in which the same categories are used but measured differently. Typically "cost" and "frequency" are alternated.

©2002 GOAL/QPC,
Six Sigma Academy

A. Major Cause Breakdowns

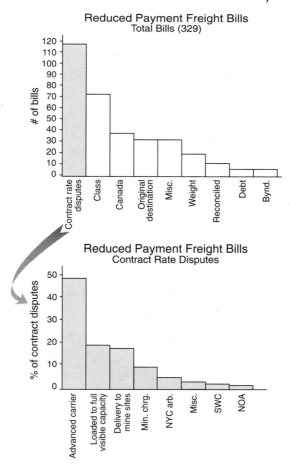

Reduced Payment Freight Bills
Total Bills (329)

# of bills

Contract rate disputes, Class, Canada, Original destination, Misc., Weight, Reconciled, Debt, Bynd.

Reduced Payment Freight Bills
Contract Rate Disputes

% of contract disputes

Advanced carrier, Loaded to full visible capacity, Delivery to mine sites, Min. chrg., NYC arb., Misc., SWC, NOA

Information provided courtesy of Goodyear

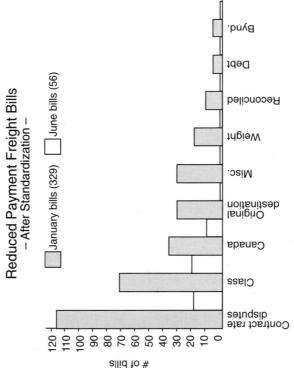

Reduced Payment Freight Bills
– After Standardization –

■ January bills (329) □ June bills (56)

Information provided courtesy of Goodyear

C. Change the Source of Data

Reason for Failed Appointments
Source of Data is: Shore-Based Command

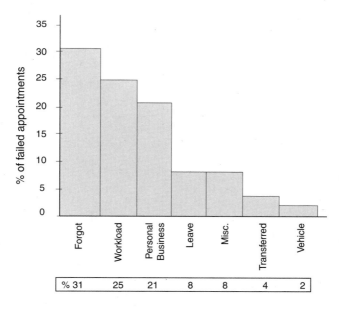

	Forgot	Workload	Personal Business	Leave	Misc.	Transferred	Vehicle
%	31	25	21	8	8	4	2

Information provided courtesy of
U.S. Navy, Naval Dental Center, San Diego

C. Change the Source of Data

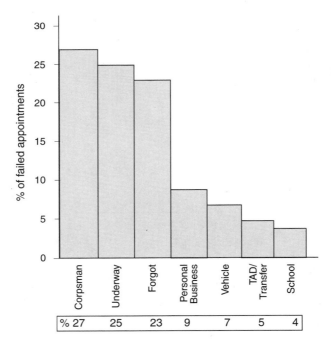

Reason for Failed Appointments
Source of Data is: Ship-Based Command

| % | 27 | 25 | 23 | 9 | 7 | 5 | 4 |

*Information provided courtesy of
U.S. Navy, Naval Dental Center, San Diego*

D. Change Measurement Scale

Field Service Customer Complaints

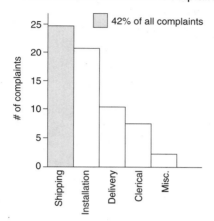

Cost to Rectify Field Service Complaints

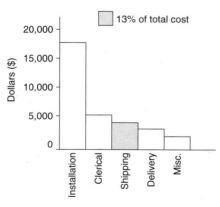

Graphical Summary

Graphical summary is a tool that can be used to summarize a collection of individual observations for a continuous variable. Quantitative inferences about the data set can be made by analyzing the many statistics that a graphical summary provides. Most common statistical programs provide some version of a graphical summary; the following summary comes from MINITAB™ software.

Graphical Summary

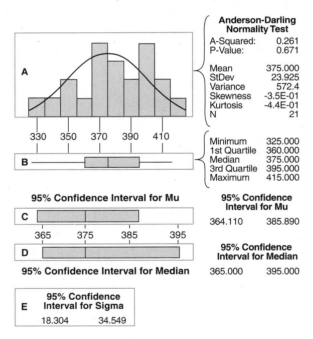

The data from the graphs shows a representative sample of the population. Described below is the information contained in the summary.

- *Figure A* - The bell-shaped curve is a normal curve (determined by the average and standard deviation of the data) and assumes normality. The bars in the histogram are the actual data. Shown to the right of the figure is the summary information. (N is the number of observations.)

  - Anderson-Darling Normality Test: If the p-value is equal to or less than a specified alpha (α) risk, there is evidence that the data does not follow a normal distribution. Because the p-value is greater than 0.05 (the typical α risk), the results of this analysis suggest that the data is normally distributed.

  - Kurtosis is a measure of the peakedness of the curve (thinner or thicker). Departures from zero can indicate non-normality. Positive kurtosis indicates a greater peak than normal. Negative kurtosis indicates a flatter peak. This example is very near zero.

- *Figure B* - This box and whisker plot displays the variability based on rank-ordering the twenty-one observations into quartiles.

- *Figure C* - The 95% Confidence Interval for Mu is an interval that can be said, with 95% certainty, to contain the true value of the population mean.

- *Figure D* - The 95% Confidence Interval for Median is an interval that can be said, with 95% certainty, to contain the true value of the population median.

• *Figure E* - The 95% Confidence Interval for Sigma is an interval that can be said, with 95% certainty, to contain the true value of the population standard deviation.

Normal Probability Plot

A normal probability plot (NPP) is used to graphically and analytically perform a hypothesis test to determine if the population distribution is normal. The NPP is a graph of calculated normal probabilities vs. a data scale. A best-fit line simulates a cumulative distribution function for the population from which the data is taken. Data that is normally distributed will appear on the plot as a straight line.

Normal Probability Plots

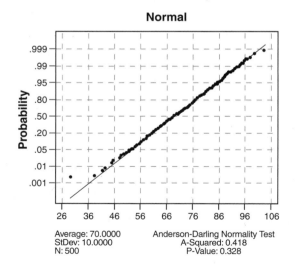

Normal

Average: 70.0000
StDev: 10.0000
N: 500

Anderson-Darling Normality Test
A-Squared: 0.418
P-Value: 0.328

One can also interpret the analytical output from an Anderson-Darling Test. If the p-value is less than the α risk, the data is not from a normal distribution.

In the example output on the previous page from MINITAB software, the plotted points fall very close to the best-fit line. In addition, the p-value (0.328) is greater than the α risk (0.05). Therefore, the data in this example is from a normal distribution.

Additional distributions have been plotted below. Notice the departure of the plotted data from the line for the positive-skewed and negative-skewed distributions. Accordingly, the p-value is less than the α risk, indicating that this data may not be from a normal parent distribution.

Negative-Skewed Distribution

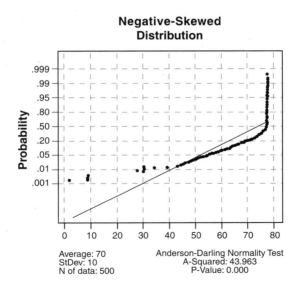

Average: 70
StDev: 10
N of data: 500

Anderson-Darling Normality Test
A-Squared: 43.963
P-Value: 0.000

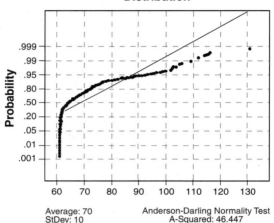

Positive-Skewed Distribution

Average: 70
StDev: 10
N of data: 500

Anderson-Darling Normality Test
A-Squared: 46.447
P-Value: 0.000

◢◣● Multi-Vari Charts

Why use it?

Multi-Vari charts are practical graphical tools that illustrate how variation in the input variables (x's) impacts the output variable (y) or response. These charts can help screen for possible sources of variation (x's). There are two types of Multi-Vari studies: 1) Passive nested studies, which are conducted without disrupting the routine of the process, and 2) Manipulated crossed studies, which are conducted by intentionally manipulating levels of the x's. Sources of variation can be either controllable and/or noise variables. Categorical x's are very typical for Multi-Vari studies (i.e., short vs. long, low vs. high, batch A vs. batch B vs. batch C). Multi-Vari studies help the organization determine where its efforts should be focused.

What does it do?

Given either historic data or data collected from a constructed sampling plan, a Multi-Vari study is a visual comparison of the effects of each of the factors by displaying, for all factors, the means at each factor level. It is an efficient graphical tool that is useful in reducing the number of candidate factors that may be impacting a response (y) down to a practical number.

Nested Designs

Sources of variation for a passive nested design might be:

- Positional (i.e., within-piece variation).
- Cyclical (i.e., consecutive piece-to-piece variation).
- Temporal (time-to-time variation, i.e., shift-to-shift or day-to-day).

Types of Variation in Nested Designs

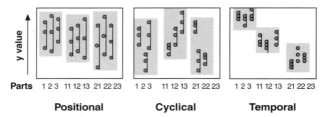

| Positional | Cyclical | Temporal |

The y axis in this figure records the measure of performance of units taken at different periods of time, in time-order sequence. Each cluster (shaded box) represents three consecutive parts, each measured in three locations. Each of the three charts represents a different process, with each process having the greatest source of variation coming from a different component. In the Positional Chart, each vertical line represents a part with the three dots recording three measurements taken on that part. The greatest variation is within the parts. In the Cyclical Chart, each cluster represents three consecutive parts. Here, the greatest variation is shown to be between consecutive parts. The third chart, the Temporal Chart, shows three clusters representing three different shifts or days, with the largest variation between the clusters.

Nested Multi-Vari Example:

In a nested Multi-Vari study, the positional readings taken were nested within a part. The positions within part were taken at random and were unique to that part; position 1 on part 1 was not the same as position 1 on part 2.

The subgroups of three "consecutive parts" were nested within a shift or day. The parts inspected were unique to that shift or day.

A sampling plan or hierarchy was created to define the parameters in obtaining samples for the study.

Sampling Plan for a Nested Design

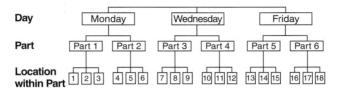

A passive nested study was conducted in which two consecutive parts (cyclical) were measured over three days (temporal). Each part was measured in three locations, which were randomly chosen on each part (positional). A nested Multi-Vari chart was then created to show the results.

Nested Multi-Vari Chart

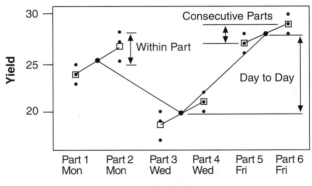

• = Individual measures
□ = Average per part
● = Average per day

Day-to-day variation appears to be the greatest source of variation, compared to the variation within part or part-to-part within a day (consecutive parts). The next step in this study would be to evaluate the process parameters that impact day-to-day variation i.e., what changes (different material lots/batches, environmental factors, etc.) are occurring day to day to affect the process.

Crossed Designs:

Sources of variation for a manipulated crossed design might be:

- Machine (A or B).
- Tool (standard or carbide).
- Coolant (off or on).

Interactions can only be observed with crossed studies. When an interaction occurs, the factors associated with the interaction must be analyzed together to see the effect of one factor's settings on the other factor's settings.

With fully crossed designs, the data may be reordered and a chart may be generated with the variables in different positions to clarify the analysis. In contrast, passive nested designs are time-based analyses and therefore must maintain the data sequence in the Multi-Vari chart.

Crossed Design Example:

A sampling plan or hierarchy for a crossed design is shown below:

Sampling Plan for a Crossed Design

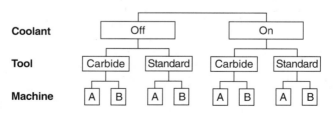

The coolant was turned "on" or "off" for each of two tools while the tools were being used on one of two machines. Every possible combination was run using the same two machines, the same two types of tools, and the same two coolant settings.

The following chart uses these sources to investigate graphically the main effects and interactions of these factors in improving surface finish (lower is better).

Crossed Multi-Vari Chart

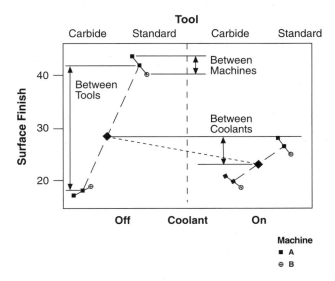

It appears that the best (lowest) value occurs with carbide tools using no coolant. The different machines have a relatively small impact. It may also be noted that when the coolant is off, there is a large difference between the two tool types. Because of the crossed nature of this study, we would conclude that there is an interaction between coolant and tool type.

Crossed Multi-Vari Chart with Different Sorting

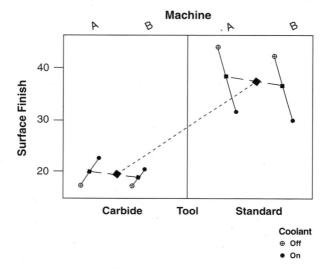

The interaction is also apparent in this second chart, which shows the same data but different sorting. Coolant "off" and "carbide tool" are again the lowest combinations. Notice how coolant "on" is now the lowest combination with the standard tool. Hence, an interaction could also be expected here.

How do I create a Multi-Vari chart?

Multi-Vari charts are easiest done with a computer, but not difficult to do by hand.

1. **Plan the Multi-Vari Study.**

    • Identify the y to be studied.

    • Determine how the y will be measured and validate the measuring system.

- Identify the potential sources of variation. For nested designs, the levels depend on passive data; for crossed designs, the levels are specifically selected for manipulation.

- Create a balanced sampling plan or hierarchy of sources. Balance refers to equal numbers of samples within the upper levels in the hierarchy (i.e., two tools for each machine). A strict balance of exactly the same number of samples for each possible combination of factors, while desirable, is not an absolute requirement. However, there must be at least one data point for each possible combination.

- Decide how to collect data in order to distinguish between the major sources of variation.

- When doing a nested study, the order of the sampling plan should be maintained to preserve the hierarchy.

2. **Take data** *in the order of production* **(not randomly).**

- Continue to collect data until 80% of the typical range of the response variable is observed (low to high). (This range may be estimated from historical data.)

Note: For fully crossed designs, a Multi-Vari study can be used to graphically look at interactions with factors that are not time dependent (in which case, runs can be randomized as in a design of experiments).

3. **Take a representative sample.**

- It is suggested that a minimum of three samples per lowest level subgroup be taken.

4. **Plot the data.**

- The y axis will represent the scaled response variable.

- Plot the positional component on a vertical line from low to high and plot the mean for each line (each piece). (**Note**: Offsetting the bar at a slight angle from vertical can improve clarity.)

- Repeat for each positional component on neighboring bars.

- Connect the positional means of each bar to evaluate the cyclical component.

- Plot the mean of all values for each cyclical group.

- Connect cyclical means to evaluate the temporal component.

- Compare components of variation for each component (largest change in y (Δy) for each component).

Tip Many computer programs will not produce charts unless the designs are balanced or have at least one data point for each combination.

Tip Each plotted point represents an average of the factor combination selected. When a different order of factors is selected, the data, while still the same, will be re-sorted. Remember, if the study is nested, the order of the hierarchy must be maintained from the top-down or bottom-up of the sampling plan.

5. **Analyze the results.**

Ask:

- Is there an area that shows the greatest source of variation?

- Are there cyclic or unexpected nonrandom patterns of variation?

- Are the nonrandom patterns restricted to a single sample or more?

- Are there areas of variation that can be eliminated (e.g., shift-to-shift variation)?

Example:

Several ribbons, one-half short and one-half long and in four colors (red, white, blue, and yellow), are studied. Three samples of each combination are taken, for a total of twenty-four data points (2 x 4 x 3). Ribbons are nested within the "length": ribbon one is unique to "short" and ribbon four is unique to "long." Length, however, is crossed with color: "short" is not unique to "blue." Length is repeated for all colors. (This example is a combination study, nested and crossed, as are many Gauge R&Rs.)

Multi-Vari Sampling Plan
Ribbon Example

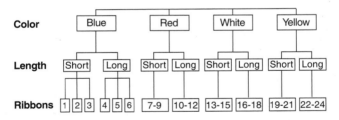

The following data set was collected. Note that there are three ribbons for each combination of length and color as identified in the "Ribbon #" column.

Color	Length	Ribbon #	Value
B	1	1	14
B	1	2	13
B	1	3	12
B	2	1	23
B	2	2	22
B	2	3	21
R	1	1	27
R	1	2	26
R	1	3	25
R	2	1	36
R	2	2	35
R	2	3	34
W	1	1	18
W	1	2	19
W	1	3	17
W	2	1	27
W	2	2	28
W	2	3	26
Y	1	1	12
Y	1	2	11
Y	1	3	10
Y	2	1	21
Y	2	2	20
Y	2	3	19

The ribbons are sorted by length, then color to get one chart.

©2002 GOAL/QPC,
Six Sigma Academy

Multi-Vari Chart for Value

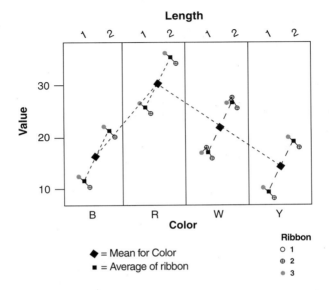

- Each observation is shown by coded circles.
- The squares are averages within a given length and color.
- Each large diamond is the average of six ribbons of both lengths within a color.
- Note the obvious pattern of the first, second, and third measured ribbons within the subgroups. The short ribbons (length = 1) consistently measure low, while the long ribbons consistently measure high, and the difference between short and long ribbons (Δy) is consistent.
- There is more variation between colors than lengths (Δy is greater between colors than between lengths).

- Also note the graph indicates that while the value of a ribbon is based upon both its color and length, longer (length = 2) ribbons are in general more valuable than short ribbons. However, a short red ribbon has higher value than a long yellow one. Caution should be taken here because not much about how the individual values vary relative to this chart is known. Other tools (e.g., hypothesis tests and DOEs) are needed for that type of analysis.

Note: Because this study has nested components associated with it, extreme caution should be used before reordering the data to generate a new chart.

⚡ Central Limit Theorem

Why use it?

The Central Limit Theorem (CLT) is a foundation for parametric hypothesis testing. Understanding this theorem furthers knowledge of how to apply inferential statistics to data.

What does it do?

The Central Limit Theorem states that the means of random samples drawn from *any* distribution with mean μ and variance σ^2 will have an approximately normal distribution with a mean equal to μ and a variance equal to σ^2/n. The CLT allows the use of confidence intervals, hypothesis testing, DOE, regression analysis, and other analytical techniques on data.

Examples:

The CLT can be better understood by reviewing examples of its application. The first example takes samples from a normal distribution; the second and third examples take samples from non-normal distributions. In each case, notice how the sampling distributions are approximately normal. Also notice that as the sample size n increases, the variation decreases and the sampling distribution tends to look more like the normal distribution.

Normal Distribution

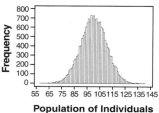

Population of Individuals

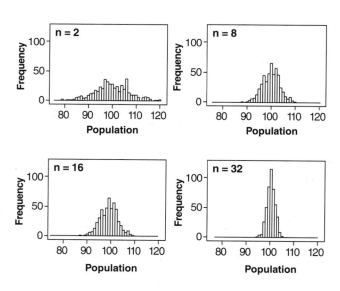

Non-normal Distribution

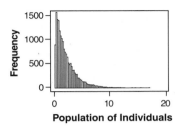

Population of Individuals

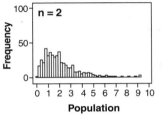

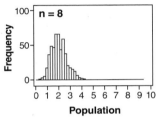

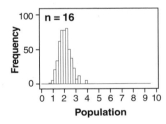

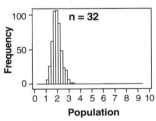

Non-normal Distribution

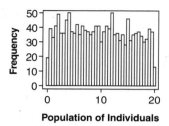

Population of Individuals

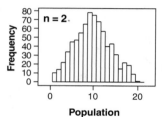

Population

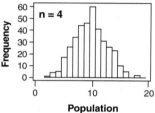

Population

 **Confidence Intervals**

Why use it?

Confidence intervals allow organizations to make estimates about population parameters (e.g., proportions, standard deviations, and averages) with a known degree of certainty.

What does it do?

In many processes, it is very costly and inefficient to measure every unit of product, service, or information produced. In these instances, a sampling plan is implemented and statistics such as the average, standard deviation, and proportion are calculated and used to make inferences about the population parameters. Unfortunately, when a known population is sampled many times, the calculated sample averages can be different even though the population is stable (as shown in the following figure).

Sample Averages

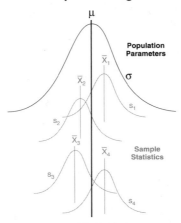

The differences in these sample averages are simply due to the nature of random sampling. Given that these differences exist, the key is to estimate the true population parameter. The confidence interval allows the organization to estimate the true population parameter with a known degree of certainty.

The confidence interval is bounded by a lower limit and upper limit that are determined by the risk associated with making a wrong conclusion about the parameter of interest. For example, if the 95% confidence interval is calculated for a subgroup of data of sample size n, and the lower confidence limit and the upper confidence limit are determined to be 85.2 and 89.3, respectively, it can be stated with 95% certainty that the true population average lies between these values. Conversely, there is a 5% risk (alpha (α) = 0.05) that this interval does not contain the true population average. The 95% confidence interval could also show that:

- Ninety-five of 100 subgroups collected with the same sample size n would contain the true population average.
- If another 100 subgroups were collected, ninety-five of the subgroups' averages would fall within the upper and lower confidence limits.

Note:

1. When sampling from a process, the samples are assumed to be randomly chosen and the subgroups are assumed to be independent.

2. Whether the true population average lies within the upper and lower confidence limits

that were calculated cannot be known. Thus, (1-confidence interval) equals the alpha risk (α), which is the risk that it does not. For a 95% confidence interval, the α risk is always 5%.

How do I do it?

Depending on the population parameter of interest, the sample statistics that are used to calculate the confidence interval subscribe to different distributions. Aspects of these distributions are used in the calculation of the confidence intervals. Listed below are the different confidence intervals, the distribution the sample statistics subscribe to, the formulas to calculate the intervals, and an example of each. Notice how these confidence intervals are affected by the sample size, n. Larger sample sizes result in tighter confidence intervals, as expected from the Central Limit Theorem.

Confidence Interval for the Mean

The confidence interval for the mean utilizes a t-distribution and can be calculated using the following formula:

$$\overline{X} - t_{\alpha/2}\left(\frac{s}{\sqrt{n}}\right) \leq \mu \leq \overline{X} + t_{\alpha/2}\left(\frac{s}{\sqrt{n}}\right)$$

Example:

A manufacturer of inserts for an automotive engine application was interested in knowing, with 90% certainty, the average strength of the inserts currently being manufactured. A sample of twenty inserts was selected and tested on a tensile tester. The average strength and standard deviation of these samples were determined to be 167,950 and 3,590 psi, respectively. The confidence interval for the mean μ would be:

$$\overline{X} - t_{\alpha/2}\left(\frac{s}{\sqrt{n}}\right) \leq \mu \leq \overline{X} + t_{\alpha/2}\left(\frac{s}{\sqrt{n}}\right)$$

$$167,950 - 1.73\left(\frac{3,590}{\sqrt{20}}\right) \leq \mu \leq 167,950 + 1.73\left(\frac{3,590}{\sqrt{20}}\right)$$

$$167,950 - 1,389 \leq \mu \leq 167,950 + 1,389$$

$$166,561 \leq \mu \leq 169,339$$

Confidence Interval for the Standard Deviation

The confidence interval for the standard deviation subscribes to a chi-square distribution and can be calculated as follows:

$$s\sqrt{\frac{(n-1)}{\chi^2_{\alpha/2,\, n-1}}} \leq \sigma \leq s\sqrt{\frac{(n-1)}{\chi^2_{1-\alpha/2,\, n-1}}}$$

A χ^2 Distribution

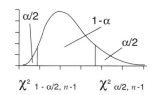

$$\chi^2_{1-\alpha/2,\, n-1} \qquad \chi^2_{\alpha/2,\, n-1}$$

s = standard deviation of a sample
χ^2 = statistical distribution
(values are listed in a statistical table)

Example:

A manufacturer of nylon fiber is interested in knowing, with 95% certainty, the amount of variability in the tenacity (a measure of strength) of a specific yarn fiber they are producing. A sample of fourteen tubes of yarn was collected, and the average tenacity and standard deviation were determined to be 2.830 and 0.341 g/denier, respectively. To calculate the 95% confidence interval for the standard deviation:

$$s\sqrt{\frac{(n-1)}{\chi^2_{\alpha/2,\, n-1}}} \leq \sigma \leq s\sqrt{\frac{(n-1)}{\chi^2_{1-\alpha/2,\, n-1}}}$$

$$0.341\sqrt{\frac{(14-1)}{24.74}} \leq \sigma \leq 0.341\sqrt{\frac{(14-1)}{5.01}}$$

$$0.247 \leq \sigma \leq 0.549$$

Caution: Some software and texts will reverse the direction of reading the table; therefore, $\chi^2_{\alpha/2,\, n-1}$ would be 5.01, not 24.74.

Confidence Interval for the Proportion Defective

The exact solution for proportion defective (p) utilizes the binomial distribution; however, in this example the normal approximation will be used. The normal approximation to the binomial may be used when np and n(1-p) are greater than or equal to five. A statistical software package will use the binomial distribution.

$$p - Z_{\alpha/2} \sqrt{\frac{p(1-p)}{n}} \leq P \leq p + Z_{\alpha/2} \sqrt{\frac{p(1-p)}{n}}$$

(This formula is best used when np and n(1-p) > 5.)

Example:

A financial company has been receiving customer phone calls indicating that their month-end financial statements are incorrect. The company would like to know, with 95% certainty, the current proportion defective for these statements. Twelve-hundred statements were sampled and fourteen of these were deemed to be defective. The 95% confidence interval for the proportion defective would be:

$$p - Z_{\alpha/2} \sqrt{\frac{p(1-p)}{n}} \leq P \leq p + Z_{\alpha/2} \sqrt{\frac{p(1-p)}{n}}$$

$$0.012 - 1.96 \sqrt{\frac{0.012(1-0.012)}{1200}} \leq P \leq 0.012 + 1.96 \sqrt{\frac{0.012(1-0.012)}{1200}}$$

$$0.012 - 0.006 \leq P \leq 0.012 + 0.006$$

$$0.006 \leq P \leq 0.018$$

$$0.60\% \leq P \leq 1.80\%$$

Note: np = 1200 (0.12) = 14.4, which is > 5 and n(1-p) = 1200 (.988) = 1185.6, which is > 5 so the normal approximation to the binomial may be used.

🏃 Hypothesis Testing

Why use it?

Hypothesis testing helps an organization:

- Determine whether making a change to a process input (x) significantly changes the output (y) of the process.
- Statistically determine if there are differences between two or more process outputs.

What does it do?

Hypothesis testing assists in using sample data to make decisions about population parameters such as averages, standard deviations, and proportions.

Testing a hypothesis using statistical methods is equivalent to making an educated guess based on the probabilities associated with being correct. When an organization makes a decision based on a statistical test of a hypothesis, it can never know for sure whether the decision is right or wrong, because of sampling variation. Regardless how many times the same population is sampled, it will never result in the same sample mean, sample standard deviation, or sample proportion. The real question is whether the differences observed are the result of changes in the population, or the result of sampling variation. Statistical tests are used because they have been designed to minimize the number of times an organization can make the wrong decision.

There are two basic types of errors that can be made in a statistical test of a hypothesis:

1. A conclusion that the population has changed when in fact it has not.

2. A conclusion that the population has not changed when in fact it has.

The first error is referred to as a type I error. The second error is referred to as a type II error. The probability associated with making a type I error is called alpha (α) or the α risk. The probability of making a type II error is called beta (β) or the β risk.

If the α risk is 0.05, any determination from a statistical test that the population has changed runs a 5% risk that it really has not changed. There is a 1 - α, or 0.95, confidence that the right decision was made in stating that the population has changed.

If the β risk is 0.10, any determination from a statistical test that there is no change in the population runs a 10% risk that there really may have been a change. There would be a 1 - β, or 0.90, "power of the test," which is the ability of the test to detect a change in the population.

A 5% α risk and a 10% β risk are typical thresholds for the risk one should be willing to take when making decisions utilizing statistical tests. Based upon the consequence of making a wrong decision, it is up to the Black Belt to determine the risk he or she wants to establish for any given test, in particular the α risk. β risk, on the other hand, is usually determined by the following:

- δ: The difference the organization wants to detect between the two population parameters. Holding all other factors constant, as the δ increases, the β decreases.

- σ: The average (pooled) standard deviation of the two populations. Holding all other factors constant, as the σ decreases, the β decreases.

- n: The number of samples in each data set. Holding all other factors constant, as the n increases, the β decreases.

- α: The alpha risk or decision criteria. Holding all other factors constant, as the α decreases, the β increases.

Most statistical software packages will have programs that help determine the proper sample size, n, to detect a specific δ, given a certain σ and defined α and β risks.

p-Value

How does an organization know if a new population parameter is different from an old population parameter? Conceptually, all hypothesis tests are the same in that a signal (δ)-to-noise (σ) ratio is calculated (δ/σ) based on the before and after data. This ratio is converted into a probability, called the p-value, which is compared to the decision criteria, the α risk. Comparing the p-value (which is the actual α of the test) to the decision criteria (the stated α risk) will help determine whether to state the system has or has not changed.

Unfortunately, a decision in a hypothesis can never conclusively be defined as a correct decision. All the hypothesis test can do is minimize the risk of making a wrong decision.

How do I do it?

A Black Belt conducting a hypothesis test is analogous to a prosecuting attorney trying a case in a court of law. The objective of the prosecuting attorney is to collect and present enough evidence to prove beyond a reasonable doubt that a defendant is guilty. If the attorney has not done so, then the jury will assume that not enough evidence has been presented to prove guilt; therefore, they will conclude the defendant is not guilty.

A Black Belt has the same objective. If the Black Belt wants to make a change to an input (x) in an existing process to determine a specified improvement in the output (y), he or she will need to collect data after the change in x to demonstrate beyond some criteria (the α risk) that the specified improvement in y was achieved.

Note: The following steps describe how to conduct a hypothesis test for a difference in means. However, these steps are the same for any hypothesis test on any other population parameter that a Black Belt may conduct.

1. **Define the problem or issue to be studied.**

2. **Define the objective.**

3. **State the null hypothesis, identified as H_0.**

   - The null hypothesis is a statement of no difference between the before and after states (similar to a defendant being not guilty in court).

$$H_0: \mu_{before} = \mu_{after}$$

The goal of the test is to either reject or not reject H_0.

4. **State the alternative hypothesis, identified as H_a.**

   - The alternative hypothesis is what the Black Belt is trying to prove and can be one of the following:

     - $H_a: \mu_{before} \neq \mu_{after}$ (a two-sided test)

     - $H_a: \mu_{before} < \mu_{after}$ (a one-sided test)

     - $H_a: \mu_{before} > \mu_{after}$ (a one-sided test)

   - The alternative chosen depends on what the Black Belt is trying to prove. In a two-sided test, it is important to detect differences from the hypothesized mean, μ_{before}, that lie on either side of μ_{before}. The α risk in a two-sided test is split on both sides of the histogram. In a one-sided test, it is only important to detect a difference on one side or the other.

5. **Determine the practical difference (δ).**

   • The practical difference is the meaningful difference the hypothesis test should detect.

6. **Establish the α and β risks for the test.**

7. **Determine the number of samples needed to obtain the desired β risk.**

   • Remember that the power of the test is $(1-\beta)$.

8. **Collect the samples and conduct the test to determine a p-value.**

   • Use a software package to analyze the data and determine a p-value.

9. **Compare the p-value to the decision criteria (α risk) and determine whether to reject H_0 in favor of H_a, or not to reject H_0.**

   • If the p-value is less than the α risk, then reject H_0 in favor H_a.

   • If the p-value is greater than the α risk, there is not enough evidence to reject H_0.

The risks associated with making an incorrect decision are described in the following table.

Decision Table

If the decision is:

If the correct answer is:	H_0	H_a
H_0	*Right Decision*	α **Risk** **Type I Error**
H_a	β **Risk** **Type II Error**	*Right Decision*

Depending on the population parameter of interest there are different types of hypothesis tests; these types are described in the following table.

Note: The table is divided into two sections: parametric and non-parametric. Parametric tests are used when the underlying distribution of the data is known or can be assumed (e.g., the data used for t-testing should subscribe to the normal distribution). Non-parametric tests are used when there is no assumption of a specific underlying distribution of the data.

Different Hypothesis Tests

	Hypothesis Test	Underlying Distribution	Purpose
Parametric (Assumes the data subscribes to a distribution)	1 Sample t-Test	Normal	Compares one sample average to a historical average or target
	2 Sample t-Test	Normal	Compares two independent sample averages
	Paired t-Test	Normal	Compares two dependent sample averages
	Test for Equal Variances	Chi-square	Compares two or more independent sample variances or standard deviations
	1 Proportion Test	Binomial	Compares one sample proportion (percentage) to a historical average or target
	2 Proportion Test	Binomial	Compares two independent proportions
	Chi-square Goodness of Fit	Chi-square	Determines whether a data set fits a known distribution
	Chi-square Test for Independence	Chi-square	Determines whether probabilities classified for one variable are associated with the classification of a second
Non-Parametric (Makes no assumption about the underlying distribution of the data)	1 Sample Sign Test	None	Compares one sample median to a historical median or target
	Mann-Whitney Test	None	Compares two independent sample medians

2 Sample t-Test Example:

A Black Belt is interested in determining whether temperature has an impact on the yield of a process. The current process runs at 100°C and results in a nominal yield of 28 kg. The Black Belt would like to change the temperature to 110°C with the hope of detecting a 3-kg increase in output. The null hypothesis is defined as:

$$H_0: \mu_{100°C} \geq \mu_{110°C} \text{ (one sided)}$$

and the alternative hypothesis is chosen as:

$$H_a: \mu_{100°C} < \mu_{110°C} \text{ (one sided)}$$

The practical difference the Black Belt would like to detect is 3 kg (an increase to 31 kg). The test is conducted with an α and β risk of 5% and 10%, respectively. To achieve a β risk of 10%, twenty-one samples will need to be collected at both 100°C and 110°C; therefore, twenty-one samples were collected at 100°C, the process temperature was changed to 110°C, and twenty-one more samples were collected. The respective averages and standard deviations were 28.2 and 3.2, and 32.4 and 3.2. The data was entered into a software program and the p-value was determined to be 0.01. After comparing the p-value (0.01) to the α risk (0.05), H_0 is rejected in favor of H_a as there is only a 1% risk in deciding H_a is greater than H_0 when compared to the initial 5% risk the Black Belt was willing to take.

2 Proportion Test Example:

A Black Belt is interested in determining whether a new method of processing forms will result in fewer defective forms. The old method resulted in 5.2% defectives. The Black Belt would like to change to a new method with the hope of reducing the percent defectives to 2.0%. The null hypothesis is defined as:

$$H_0: P_{old\ method} \leq P_{new\ method}$$

and the alternative hypothesis is chosen as:

$$H_a: P_{old\ method} > P_{new\ method}$$

The practical difference the Black Belt would like to detect is a 3.2% reduction. The test will be conducted with an α and β risk of 5% and 10%, respectively. To achieve a β risk of 10%, 579 forms will need to be collected at the old and new methods; therefore, 579 samples were collected at the old process, the new method was implemented, and 579 more samples were collected. The respective percentages were 5.2% (thirty defectives) and 2.9% (seventeen defectives). The data was entered into a software program and the p-value was determined to be 0.026. Comparing the p-value (0.026) to the α risk (0.05) results in a conclusion that H_0 should be rejected.

🏃 Transforming Data

Why use it?

Many graphical and statistical analysis tools assume the distribution of data or residuals is normal and of equal variance over the range of the analysis. If the distribution is non-normal, then the analysis may be misleading or incorrect due to the violation of the normality and equal variance assumptions. A transformation function can often be used to convert the data closer to a normal distribution to meet the assumptions and allow for a determination of statistical significance. Transformation use may be indicated by non-random patterns in the residuals of a regression, ANOVA, or DOE analysis.

What does it do?

A transformation function converts a non-normal distribution to a normal distribution. Caution must be used by the analyst in interpreting transformed data that has no physical significance.

How do I do it? 🏃

Before transforming data, it is important to see if the sample size of data is large enough to determine normality (typically ≥ thirty samples) and if the sample is representative of the process being measured. It is also important to ensure that multiple populations are not included in the sample (multiple modes or outliers may be indicative of this). Finally, the process being measured must be considered; a normal distribution profile would be characterized by data that are just as likely to be below the mean as above the mean, and that are more likely to be close to the mean than farther away from the mean.

Once it has been determined that the data or residuals are non-normal, a transformation function is used to transform the data. The same test for normality should then be performed on the transformed data. If the new distribution is normal, then an analysis that assumes normality can be used on the transformed data. If the new distribution is not normal, then the data can be transformed using a different type of transformation, or the data should be reviewed to determine if more than one population is represented or a non-parametric analysis can be conducted.

Data Transformation Types

It is often difficult to determine which transformation function to use for the data given. Many people decide which function to use by trial and error, using the standard transformation functions shown on the next page. For each function or combination of functions, the transformed data can be checked for normality using the Anderson-Darling test for normality.

A transformation function can incorporate any one or combination of the following equations, or may use additional ones not listed.

Standard Transformation Functions

- Square Root: $\sqrt{x}$
- Logarithmic: $\log 10\ x$, $\ln x$, etc.
- Reciprocal of data: $1/x$
- Square of data: x^2

There is also benefit in transforming specific distributions such as count data. This type of data often has a nonconstant variance (Poisson distribution). Recommended transformations are listed below:

- Square Root: $\sqrt{c}$
- Freeman-Tukey modification to the square root:

$$\left[\sqrt{c} + \sqrt{c+1}\ \right]/2$$

Another frequently encountered situation requiring transformation occurs when dealing with attribute data. Recommended transformations include:

- Arcsin $\sqrt{p}$
- Freeman-Tukey modification to arcsin:

$$\left[\arcsin\sqrt{\frac{np}{n+1}} + \arcsin\sqrt{\frac{np+1}{n+1}}\right]/2$$

By knowing the physics behind a process, the Black Belt can determine the appropriate function that describes the process. This function can be used to transform the data.

Once the transformation function is found for a given set of data, it can be used for additional data collected from the same process. Once a process has been modified, however, the distribution may change and become normal or a different type of non-normal distribution. A new transformation function may then be needed.

If choosing a transformation is difficult, many software programs will perform a Box-Cox transformation on the data. Some common Box-Cox transformations are listed in the following table.

Box-Cox Transformations

Use y^λ when $\lambda \neq 0$ and $\ln(y)$ when $\lambda = 0$.

If the lambda value is:	Then the transformation value will be:
2	y^2
0.05	$y^{0.05}$
0	ln (y)
-0.5	$1/y^{0.5}$
-1	$1/y$
1	No transformation required

The table can be used to assess the appropriateness of the transformation. For example, the 95% confidence interval for lambda can be used to determine whether the optimum lambda value is "close" to 1, because a lambda of 1 indicates that a transformation should not be done. If the optimum lambda is close to 1, very little would be gained by performing the transformation.

As another example, if the optimum lambda is "close" to 0.5, the square root of the data could simply be calculated, because this transformation is simple and understandable.

Note: In some cases, one of the closely competing values of lambda may end up having a slightly smaller standard deviation than the estimate chosen.

Example:

A data set was evaluated and discovered to be non-normally distributed. The distribution was positively skewed because the exaggerated tail was in the positive direction.

Non-normally Distributed Data

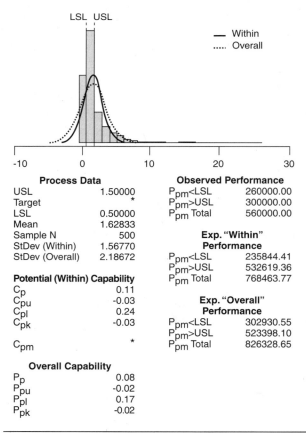

Process Data		Observed Performance	
USL	1.50000	P_{pm}<LSL	260000.00
Target	*	P_{pm}>USL	300000.00
LSL	0.50000	P_{pm} Total	560000.00
Mean	1.62833		
Sample N	500	**Exp. "Within"**	
StDev (Within)	1.56770	**Performance**	
StDev (Overall)	2.18672	P_{pm}<LSL	235844.41
		P_{pm}>USL	532619.36
		P_{pm} Total	768463.77

Potential (Within) Capability		
C_p	0.11	**Exp. "Overall"**
C_{pu}	-0.03	**Performance**
C_{pl}	0.24	P_{pm}<LSL 302930.55
C_{pk}	-0.03	P_{pm}>USL 523398.10
C_{pm}	*	P_{pm} Total 826328.65

Overall Capability	
P_p	0.08
P_{pu}	-0.02
P_{pl}	0.17
P_{pk}	-0.02

The same data set was evaluated using a Box-Cox transformation analysis. The Box-Cox transformation plot is shown below.

Box-Cox Transformation Plot

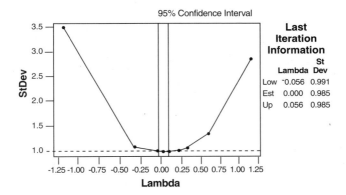

95% Confidence Interval

	Last Iteration Information	
	Lambda	St Dev
Low	⁻0.056	0.991
Est	0.000	0.985
Up	0.056	0.985

In this example, the best estimate for lambda is zero or the natural log. (In any practical situation, the Black Belt would want a lambda value that corresponds to an understandable transformation, such as the square root (a lambda of 0.5) or the natural log (a lambda of 0).) Zero is a reasonable choice because it falls within the 95% confidence interval and happens to be the "best" estimate of lambda. Therefore, the natural log transformation will be used.

After performing the recommended transformation on the data set, a test for normality was done to validate the transformation. (The normal probability plot for this data is shown on the next page.)

Normal Probability Plot

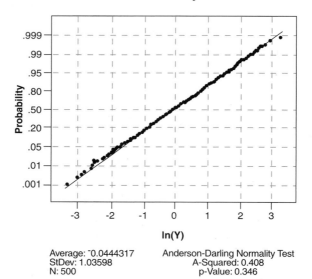

Average: ⁻0.0444317
StDev: 1.03598
N: 500

Anderson-Darling Normality Test
A-Squared: 0.408
p-Value: 0.346

The normal probability plot of the transformed data can be graphically interpreted by the fit of the data to a straight line, or analytically interpreted from the results of the Anderson-Darling test for normality. The p-value (0.346) is greater than the α risk we are willing to take, indicating that there is sufficient evidence that the transformed distribution is normally distributed.

The original lognormal capability data has been transformed into the normal distribution shown on the next page. (The * in the graphic indicates transformed data. For example, the actual USL is 1.50; however, the transformed USL is 0.405.)

Transformed Capability Data

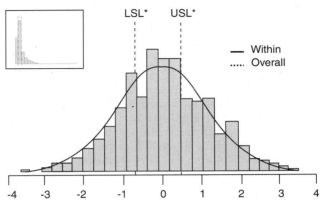

LSL* USL*

— Within
..... Overall

-4 -3 -2 -1 0 1 2 3 4

Process Data

USL	1.50000
USL*	0.40547
Target	*
Target*	*
LSL	0.50000
LSL*	-0.69315
Mean	1.62833
Mean*	-0.04443
Sample N	500
StDev (Within)	1.56770
StDev* (Within)	1.02145
StDev (Overall)	2.18672
StDev* (Overall)	1.03650

Potential (Within) Capability

C_p	0.18
C_{pu}	0.15
C_{pl}	0.21
C_{pk}	0.15
C_{pm}	*

Overall Capability

P_p	0.18
P_{pu}	0.14
P_{pl}	0.21
P_{pk}	0.14

Observed Performance

P_{pm}<LSL	260000.00
P_{pm}>USL	300000.00
P_{pm} Total	560000.00

Exp. "Within" Performance

P_{pm}<LSL*	262683.84
P_{pm}>USL*	329805.84
P_{pm} Total	592489.68

Exp. "Overall" Performance

P_{pm}<LSL*	265699.92
P_{pm}>USL*	332124.86
P_{pm} Total	597824.78

The potential and overall capabilities are now more accurate for the process at hand. The use of non-normal data may result in an erroneous calculation of predicted proportion out of the specified units. When transforming capability data, remember that any specification limit must also be transformed. (Most software packages will perform this automatically.)

Notice from a comparison of the before and after capability outputs that we are only slightly more capable than our original estimate with the lognormal data. There is excessive variation in the process. The primary focus of the Black Belt should be to identify and correct the sources of this variation.

 **Correlation and Regression**

Correlation

Why use it?
Correlation is used to determine the strength of linear relationships between two process variables. It allows the comparison of an input to an output, two inputs against each other, or two outputs against each other.

What does it do?
Correlation measures the degree of association between two independent continuous variables. However, even if there is a high degree of correlation, this tool does not establish causation. For example, the number of skiing accidents in Colorado is highly correlated with sales of warm clothing, but buying warm clothes did not cause the accidents.

How do I do it?
Correlation can be analyzed by calculating the Pearson product moment correlation coefficient (r). This coefficient is calculated as follows:

$$r_{xy} = \frac{\frac{1}{n-1} \sum_{i=1}^{n} (x_i - \bar{X})(y_i - \bar{y})}{S_x S_y}$$

Where S_x and S_y are the sample standard deviations.

The resulting value will be a number between -1 and +1. The higher the absolute value of r, the stronger the correlation. A value of zero means there is no correlation. A strong correlation is characterized by a tight distribution of plotted pairs about a best-fit line. It should be noted that correlation does not measure the slope of the best-fit line; it measures how close the data are to the best-fit line. A negative r implies that as one variable (x^2) increases, the other variable (x^1) decreases.

Weak Negative Correlation

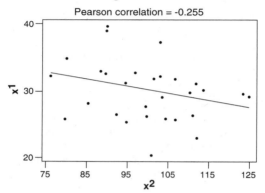

Pearson correlation = -0.255

Strong Negative Correlation

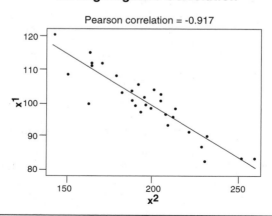

Pearson correlation = -0.917

A positive r implies that as one variable (x^3) increases, the other variable (x^1) also increases.

Weak Positive Correlation

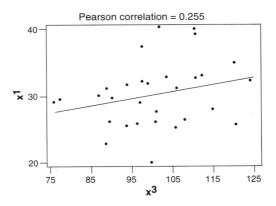

Pearson correlation = 0.255

Strong Positive Correlation

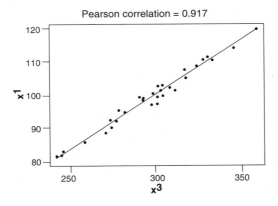

Pearson correlation = 0.917

As stated earlier, correlation is a measure of the linear relationship between two variables. A strong relationship other than linear can exist, yet r can be close to zero.

Strong Non-Linear Relationship

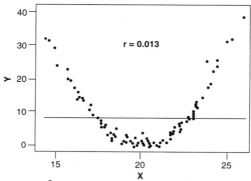

$r = 0.013$

Regression

Why use it?

Regression measures the strength of association between independent factor(s) (also called predictor variable(s) or regressors) and a dependent variable (also called a response variable). For simple or multiple linear regression, the dependent variable must be a continuous variable. Predictor variables can be continuous or discrete, but must be independent of one another. Discrete variables may be coded, discrete levels (dummy variables $(0, 1)$ or effects coding $(-1, +1)$).

- *Simple linear regression* relates a single x to a y. It has a single regressor (x) variable and its model is linear with respect to coefficients (a).

  Examples:
  $$y = a_0 + a_1x + error$$
  $$y = a_0 + a_1x + a_2 x^2 + a_3 x^3 + error$$

©2002 GOAL/QPC, Six Sigma Academy

Note: "Linear" refers to the coefficients a_0, a_1, a_2, etc. In the second example, the relationship between x and y is a cubic polynomial in nature, but the model is still linear with respect to the coefficients.

- *Multiple linear regression* relates multiple x's to a y. It has multiple regressor (x) variables such as x_1, x_2, and x_3. Its model is linear with respect to coefficients (b).

  Example:

  $$y = b_0 + b_1 x_1 + b_2 x_2 + b_3 x_3 + \text{error}$$

- *Binary logistic regression* relates x's to a y that can only have a dichotomous (one of two mutually exclusive outcomes such as pass / fail, on / off, etc.) value. (For more information on this subject, see the binary logistic regression chapter in this book.)

- Other regression equations such as nonlinear regressions are possible but are beyond the scope of this book and are best performed by computer programs. Other logistic regressions (which use discrete data) such as ordinal (three or more categories of natural order such as mild, medium, and hot) or nominal (three or more categories of no natural order such as yellow, blue, and red) are also possible but are similarly beyond the scope of this book.

How do I do simple regression?

1. Determine which relationship will be studied.

2. Collect data on the x and y variables.

3. Set up a fitted line plot by charting the independent variable on the x axis and the dependent variable on the y axis.

4. Create the fitted line.

   - If creating the fitted line plot by hand, draw a straight line through the values that keep the least amount of total space between the line and the individual plotted points (a "best fit").

- If using a computer program, compute and plot this line via the "least squares method."

Fitted Line Plot

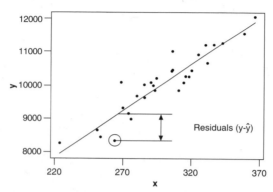

5. Compute the correlation coefficient r, using the equation defined earlier in this chapter.

6. Determine the slope or y intercept of the line by using the equation y = mx + b.

   - The y intercept (b) is the point on the y axis through which the "best fitted line" passes (at this point, x = 0).

   - The slope of the line (m) is computed as the change in y divided by the change in x (m = $\Delta y / \Delta x$). The slope, m, is also known as the coefficient of the predictor variable, x.

7. Calculate the residuals.

   - The difference between the predicted response variable (called the fits, $\hat{y}$) for any given x and the experimental value or actual response (y) is called the residual (e = y -$\hat{y}$). The residual is used

---

 ©2002 GOAL/QPC,
Six Sigma Academy

to determine if the model is a good one to use. The estimated standard deviation of the residuals is a measure of the error term about the regression line.

8. **To determine significance, perform a t-test (with the help of a computer) and calculate a p-value for each factor.**

   • A p-value less than α (usually 0.05) will indicate a statistically significant relationship.

9. **Analyze the entire model for significance using ANOVA, which displays the results of an F-test with an associated p-value.**

10. **Calculate R^2 and R^2_{adj}.**

   • R^2, the coefficient of determination, is the square of the correlation coefficient and measures the proportion of variation that is explained by the model. Ideally, R^2 should be equal to one, which would indicate zero error.

$$R^2 = SS_{regression} \ / \ SS_{total}$$
$$= (SS_{total} \ - SS_{error} \ ) \ / \ SS_{total}$$
$$= 1 - [SS_{error} \ / \ SS_{total} \ ]$$

   Where SS = the sum of the squares.

   • R^2_{adj} is a modified measure of R^2 that takes into account the number of terms in the model and the number of data points.

$$R^2_{adj} = 1 - [SS_{error} \ / \ (n-p)] \ / \ [SS_{total} \ / \ (n-1)]$$

   Where n = number of data points and p = number of terms in the model. The number of terms in the model also includes the constant.

   Note: Unlike R^2, R^2_{adj} can become smaller when added terms provide little new information and as the number of model terms gets closer to the total sample size. Ideally, R^2_{adj} should be maximized and as close to R^2 as possible.

Conclusions should be validated, especially when historical data has been used.

Example:

A Black Belt wants to determine if there is a relationship between the amount of shelf space allocated for a specific product and the sales volume for that same product. She investigates thirty different stores of the same chain, all with similar demographics. Data is collected comparing shelf space allocated (x) to sales (y). Using a computer program to run an ANOVA shows the following result:

Analysis of Variance

Source	DF	SS	MS	F	P
Regression	1	23.3107	23.3107	181.234	0.000
Error	28	3.6014	0.1286		
Total	29	26.9121			

$s = 0.3586$, $n = 30$, & # of terms, $p = 2$

$R^2 = SS_{regression}/SS_{total} = 23.3107 / 26.9121 = 86.6\%$
Note: Square the correlation coefficient (r) and compare.
86.6% of variation in sales can be attributed to shelf space.

$$R^2_{adj} = 1 - [SS_{error} / (n-p)] / [SS_{total}/ (n-1)]$$
$$= 1 - [3.6014 / (30 - 2)] / [26.9121 / (30 - 1)]$$
$$= 1 - 0.1286 / 0.9280 = 86.1\%$$

DF = Degrees of freedom
SS = Sum of squares
MS = Mean square
F = F ratio
s = Standard deviation
P = p-value

Correlation analysis shows a strong positive correlation (r = +0.931).

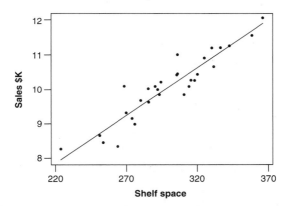

**Strong Positive Correlation
Between Shelf Space and Sales**
b = 1.7712 and m = 0.0276, which implies
that for each unit of shelf space, sales increase $27.60.
Sales $K = 1.77121 + 0.0276075 shelf space

Correlation, r = + 0.931
R^2 = 86.6%
R^2_{adj} = 86.1%

How do I do more advanced techniques such as multiple regression and residual analysis?

Using a computer program, a similar method is used in performing multiple regression, but the x axis can no longer represent a single factor.

1. **After obtaining a prediction equation (y = mx + b), analyze the residuals to validate the assumptions for regression.**

   Residuals should:

   • Be normally distributed with a mean of zero.

- Show no pattern (i.e., be random).

- Have constant variance when plotted against any regression factor or predicted values / fits.

- Be independent of the predictor variables (x's).

- Be independent of each other.

2. **Check for patterns.**

   - Any significant pattern seen may be an indication of a missed factor. Add extra factors, try a quadratic multiplier, or modify the formula or transform the data and reanalyze the model.

3. **Once any patterns are eliminated, confirm that multicolinearity is minimized.**

   - Multicolinearity is a measure of correlation between the dependent variables and can be quantified with the Variation Inflation Factor. (Ideally, VIF < 5.) (More detail about VIF goes beyond the scope of this book. For detailed information, see *Introduction to Linear Regression Analysis* by D.C. Montgomery and E.A. Peck.)

4. **Calculate R^2 and R^2_{adj}.**

   Tip Make sure that the R^2_{adj} is the highest value obtainable with the fewest (simplest model) number of variables. Best subsets and stepwise regression are methodologies that help this optimizing effort.

Example:

A Black Belt wants to evaluate the effect of three continuous factors (temperature, pressure, and dwell) on the yield of a process.

Data from twenty-one runs is collected and, as shown in the table below, all three factors are statistically significant, giving a regression formula of four terms ($n = 21$ and $p = 4$). This computer-generated output provides the ANOVA table and p-values, confirming the validity of our model (F-test) and its component factors (t-tests).

ANOVA and p-Values

Analysis of Variance

Source	DF	SS	MS	F	P
Regression	3	2572.87	857.62	52.81	0.000
Residual Error	17	276.08	16.24		
Total	20	2848.95			

Predictor	Coef	SE Coef	T	P	
Constant	-25.402	9.761	-2.60	0.019	
Temp	0.13519	0.04735	2.86	0.011	
Pressure	0.33252	0.08038	4.14	0.001	
Dwell	0.11444	0.05319	2.15	0.046	

Note: All three factors are significant because they are less than the α risk (0.05) we are willing to take.

Yield = -25.4 + 0.135 Temp + 0.333 Pressure + 0.114 Dwell

$R^2 = SS_{regression}/SS_{total} = 2572.87 / 2848.95 = 90.3\%$

$R^2_{adj} = 1 - [SS_{error} / (n\text{-}p)] / [SS_{total} / (n\text{-}1)]$
$= 1 - [276.08 / (21 - 4)] / [2848.95 / (21 - 1)]$
$= 1 - 16.24 / 142.45 = 88.6\%$

The residuals were analyzed to validate the assumptions for regression / ANOVA.

Residuals Analysis

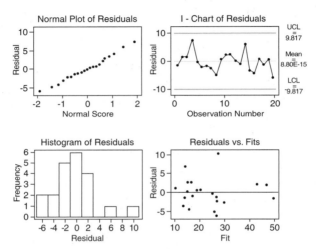

Some computer programs will scan the residuals and identify any standardized residual over a set limit (typically two). This is essentially an identification of potential outliers possibly worth investigating.

Standardized Residual = Residual ÷ Standard Deviation of the Residual.

Binary Logistic Regression

Why use it?

Binary logistic regression (BLR) is used to establish a $y = f(x)$ relationship when the dependent variable (y) is binomial or dichotomous. Similar to regression, it explores the relationships between one or more predictor variables and a binary response. BLR enables the Black Belt to predict the probability of future events belonging to one group or another (i.e., pass/fail, profitable/non-profitable, or purchase/not purchase).

What does it do?

The predictor variables (x's) can be either continuous or discrete, just as for any problem using regression. However, the response variable has only two possible values (e.g., pass/fail, etc.). Because regression analysis requires a continuous response variable that is not bounded, this must be corrected. This is accomplished by first converting the response from events (e.g., pass/fail) to the probability of one of the events, or p. Thus if p = Probability(pass), then p can take on any value from 0 to 1. This conversion results in a continuous response, but one that is still bounded. An additional transformation is required to make the response both continuous and unbounded. This is called the link function. The most common link function is the "logit," which is explained below.

$$Y = \beta_0 + \beta_1 x$$

We need a continuous, unbounded Y.

$0 < p < 1$ $\quad 0 < \dfrac{p}{1 - p} < \infty$ $\qquad \dfrac{p}{1 - p}$ is called the "odds"

$-\infty < \ln\left(\dfrac{p}{1-p}\right) < +\infty$ $\qquad \ln\left(\dfrac{p}{1-p}\right)$ is the "logit"

BLR fits sample data to an S-shaped logistic curve. The curve represents the probability of the event.

BLR Fits Data to a Probability Curve

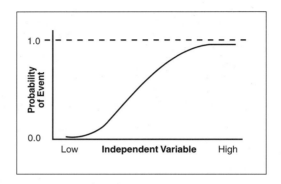

At low levels of the independent variable (x), the probability approaches zero. As the predictor variable increases, the probability increases to a point where the slope decreases. At high levels of the independent variable, the probability approaches 1.

The following two examples fit probability curves to actual data. The curve on the top represents the "best fit." The curve through the data on the bottom contains a zone of uncertainty where events and non-events (1's and 0's) overlap.

Probability Curve Examples

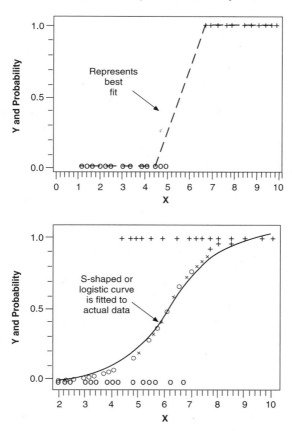

If the probability of an event, p, is greater than 0.5, binary logistic regression would predict a "yes" for the event to occur. The probability of an event *not* occurring is described as (1-p). The odds, or p/(1-p), compares the probability of an event occurring to the probability of it not occurring. The logit, or "link" function, represents the relationship between x and y.

$$\ln \left(\frac{P_{event}}{P_{non\text{-}event}} \right) = \beta_0 + \beta_1 x_1 \cdots + \beta_n x_n = \ln \left(\frac{p}{1\text{-}p} \right)$$

$$P_{(event)} = \frac{e^{\,f}}{1+e^{f}} \text{ where } f = \beta_0 + \beta_1 x$$

How do I do it?

1. Define the problem and the question(s) to be answered.

2. Collect the appropriate data in the right quantity.

3. Hypothesize a model.

4. Analyze the data.

   • Many statistical software packages are available to help analyze data.

5. Check the model for goodness of fit.

6. Check the residuals for violations of assumptions.

7. Modify the model, if required, and repeat.

Interpreting the results of BLR

Most statistical software will estimate coefficients, which represent the change in the logit, or $\ln(p/(1-p))$, corresponding to a one-unit change in an x variable, if all other x variables are held constant. Also, for each x variable, one can obtain an "odds ratio." This is the ratio of the "odds" with a particular x at some base value (x_0) compared to the "odds" if the same x variable were increased by 1 unit (i.e., $x = x_0 + 1$). The "odds ratio" for each x variable is calculated directly from the coefficient (β) for that x (i.e., it is e^β).

Positive coefficients mean that the predicted probability of the event increases as the input (x) increases. Positive coefficients also result in an odds ratio that is > 1.

Negative coefficients mean that the predicted probability of the event decreases as the input (x) increases. Negative coefficients also result in an odds ratio that is < 1.

A coefficient of 0 means that there is no change in the predicted probability of the event as the input (x) increases. This also results in an odds ratio that is = 1. Variables with coefficients close to 0 or odds ratios close to 1 can be removed from the model.

In the following example, a value of 1.0 means the event is a "failure."

Using a Probability Curve to Predict an Event

$$\ln\left(\frac{p}{1-p}\right) = \beta_0 + \beta_1 x \qquad X_{50} = \frac{-\beta_0}{\beta_1} = \frac{7.092}{0.12463} = 56.9$$

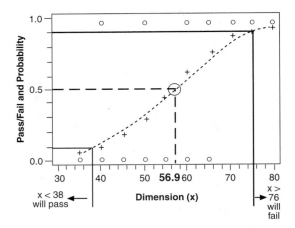

A dimension of 56.9 has a 50% chance of failing. As the dimension increases, it is more likely to cause a failure. Two other dimensions have also been highlighted: a dimension of 38 only has a 10% chance of failing while a dimension of 76 has a 90% probability of failure.

⚡ Design of Experiments

Why use it?

Design of experiments (DOE) is used to understand the effects of the factors and interactions that impact the output of a process. As a battery of tests, a DOE is designed to methodically build understanding and enhance the predictability of a process.

Note: There are many kinds of DOEs. This book will only consider full and fractional factorial DOEs. These DOEs emphasize the role that interactions and noise play in understanding a process. A brief overview of other DOE designs is listed at the end of this chapter.

What does it do?

A DOE investigates a list of potential factors whose variation might impact the process output. These factors can be derived from a variety of sources including process maps, FMEAs, Multi-Vari studies, Fishbone Diagrams, brainstorming techniques, and Cause and Effect Matrices.

The types of DOEs include:

- *Screening DOEs*, which ignore most of the higher order interaction effects so that the team can reduce the candidate factors down to the most important ones.

- *Characterization DOEs*, which evaluate main factors and interactions to provide a prediction equation. These equations can range from 2^k designs up to general linear models with multiple factors at multiple levels. Some software packages readily evaluate nonlinear effects using center points and also allow for the use of blocking in 2^k analyses.

- *Optimizing DOEs*, which use more complex designs such as Response Surface Methodology or iterative simple designs such as evolutionary operation or plant experimentation to determine the optimum set of factors.

- *Confirming DOEs*, where experiments are done to ensure that the prediction equation matches reality.

Understanding DOEs requires an explanation of certain concepts and terms.

- A *balanced design* will have an equal number of runs at each combination of the high and low settings for each factor.

- Two columns in a design matrix are *orthogonal* if the sum of the products of their elements within each row is equal to zero.

  Note: When a factorial experiment is balanced, the design is said to be completely orthogonal. The Pearson correlation coefficient of all of the factor and interaction columns will be zero.

- *Aliasing* (which is also referred to as confounding) occurs when the analysis of a factor or interaction cannot be unambiguously determined because the factor or interaction settings are identical to another factor or interaction, or is a linear combination of other factors or interactions. As a result, the Black Belt might not know which factor or interaction is responsible for the change in the output value. Note that aliasing / confounding can be additive, where two or more insignificant effects add and give a false impression of statistical validity. Aliasing can also offset two important effects and essentially cancel them out.

- The principle of *design projection* states that if the outcome of a fractional factorial design has insignificant terms, the insignificant terms can be removed from the model, thereby reducing the design. For example, determining the effect of four factors for a full factorial design would normally require sixteen runs (a 2^4 design). Because of resource limitations, only a half fraction (a $2^{(4-1)}$ design) consisting of eight trials can be run. If the analysis showed that one of the main effects (and associated interactions) was insignificant, then that factor could be removed from the model and the design analyzed as a full factorial design. A half fraction has therefore become a full factorial. (**Note:** This procedure requires the experiment design to be orthogonal.)

- *Blocking* allows the team to study the effects of noise factors and remove any potential effects resulting from a known noise factor. For example, an experimental design may require a set of eight runs to be complete, but there is only enough raw material in a lot to perform four runs. There is a concern that different results may be obtained with the different lots of material. To prevent these differences, should they exist, from influencing the results of the experiment, the runs are divided into two halves with each being balanced and orthogonal. Thus, the DOE is done in two halves or "blocks" with "material lot" as the blocking factor. (Because there is not enough material to run all eight experiments with one lot, some runs will have to be done with each material anyway.) Analysis will determine if there is a statistically significant difference in these two blocks. If there is no difference, the blocks can be removed from the model and the data treated as a whole. Blocking is a way of determining which trials to run with each lot so that any effect from the different material will not influence the decisions made about the effects of the factors being explored. If the blocks are significant, then the experimenter was correct in the choice of blocking factor and the noise due to the blocking factor was minimized. This may also lead to more experimentation on the blocking factor.

- *Resolution* is the amount and structure of aliasing of factors and interactions in an experimental design. Roman numerals are used to indicate the degree of aliasing, with Resolution III being the most confounded. A full factorial design has no terms that are aliased. The numeral indicates the aliasing pattern. A Resolution III has main effects and two-way interactions confounded (1+2 = III). A Resolution V has one-way and four-way interactions as well as two-way and three-way interactions aliased (1+4 = V = 2+3).

- *Randomization* is a technique to distribute the effect of unknown noise variables over all the factors. Because some noise factors may change over time, any factors whose settings are not randomized could be confounded with these time-dependent elements. Examples of factors that change over time are tool wear, operator fatigue, process bath concentrations, and changing temperatures throughout the day.

- A *random factor* is any factor whose settings (such as any speed within an operating range) could be randomly selected, as opposed to a *fixed factor* whose settings (such as the current and proposed levels) are those of specific interest to the Black Belt. Fixed factors are used when an organization wishes to investigate the effects of particular settings or, at most, the inference space enclosed by them. Random factors are used when the organization wishes to draw conclusions about the entire population of levels.

- The *inference space* is the operating range of the factors. It is where the factor's range is used to infer an output to a setting not used in the design. Normally, it is assumed that the settings of the factors within the minimum and maximum experimental settings are acceptable levels to use in a prediction equation. For example, if factor A has low and high settings of five and ten units, it is reasonable to make predictions when the factor is at a setting of six. However, predictions at a value of thirteen cannot and should not be attempted because this setting is outside the region that was explored. (For a 2^k design, a check for curvature should be done prior to assuming linearity between the high and low outputs.)

- A *narrow inference* utilizes a small number of test factors and/or factor levels or levels that are close together to minimize the noise in a DOE. One example of a narrow inference is having five machines, but doing a DOE on just one machine to minimize the noise variables of machines and operators.

- A *broad inference* utilizes a large number of the test factors and/or factor levels or levels that are far apart, recognizing that noise will be present. An example of a broad inference is performing a DOE on all five machines. There will be more noise, but the results more fully address the entire process.

- A *residual* is a measure of error in a model. A prediction equation estimates the output of a process at various levels within the inference space. These predicted values are called fits. The residual is the difference between a fit and an actual experimentally observed data point.

- *Residual analysis* is the graphical analysis of residuals to determine if a pattern can be detected. If the prediction equation is a good model, the residuals will be independently and normally distributed with a mean of zero and a constant variance.

Nonrandom patterns indicate that the underlying assumptions for the use of ANOVA have not been met. It is important to look for nonrandom and/or non-normal patterns in the residuals. These types of patterns can often point to potential solutions. For example, if the residuals have more than one mode, there is most likely a missing factor. If the residuals show trends or patterns vs. the run order, there is a time-linked factor.

- A DOE may use *continuous and/or discrete factors*. A continuous factor is one (such as feed rate) whose levels can vary continuously, while a discrete factor will have a predetermined finite number of levels (such as supplier A or supplier B). Continuous factors are needed when true curvature/center point analysis is desired.

- The *sparsity of effects principle* states that processes are usually driven by main effects and low-order interactions.

How do I do a DOE?

In general, the steps to perform a DOE include:

1. **Document the initial information.**

2. **Verify the measurement systems.**

3. **Determine if baseline conditions are to be included in the experiment. (This is usually desirable.)**

4. **Make sure clear responsibilities are assigned for proper data collection.**

5. **Always perform a pilot run to verify and improve data collection procedures.**

6. **Watch for and record any extraneous sources of variation.**

7. **Analyze data promptly and thoroughly.**

8. Always run one or more verification runs to confirm results (i.e., go from a narrow to broad inference).

How do I set up an experiment? 🏃

1. State the practical problem.

   • For example, a practical problem may be "Improve yield by investigating factor A and factor B. Use an α of 0.05."

2. State the factors and levels of interest.

   • For example, factors and levels of interest could be defined as, "Set coded values for factors A and B at -1 and +1."

3. Select the appropriate design and sample size based on the effect to be detected.

4. Create an experimental data sheet with the factors in their respective columns.

   • Randomize the experimental runs in the data sheet. Conduct the experiment and record the results.

How do I analyze data 🏃
from an experiment?

5. Construct an Analysis of Variance (ANOVA) table for the full model.

6. Review the ANOVA table and eliminate effects with p-values above α.

   • *Remove these one at a time,* starting with the highest order interactions.

7. Analyze the residual plots to ensure that the model fits.

8. Investigate the significant interactions (p-value $< α$).

   • Assess the significance of the highest order interactions first. (For two-way interactions, an interactions plot may be used to efficiently determine optimum settings. For graphical analysis to determine settings for three-way interactions, it is necessary to evaluate two or more interactions plots simultaneously.)

• Once the highest order interactions are interpreted, analyze the next set of lower order interactions.

9. **Investigate the significant main effects (p-value < α).**

(**Note:** If the level of the main effect has already been set as a result of a significant interaction, this step is not needed.)

• The use of the main effects plots is an efficient way to identify these values. Main effects that are part of statistically valid interactions must be kept in the model, regardless of whether or not they are statistically valid themselves. Care must be taken because, due to interactions, the settings chosen from a main effects plot may sometimes lead to a suboptimized solution. If there is a significant interaction, use an interaction plot, as shown in the following chart.

Main Effects and Interactions Plot

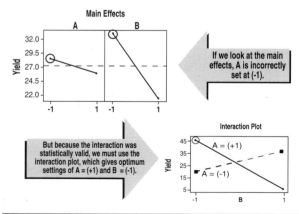

©2002 GOAL/QPC,
Six Sigma Academy

10. State the mathematical model obtained.

- For a 2^k design, the coefficients for each factor and interaction are one-half of their respective effects. Therefore, the difference in the mean of the response from the low setting to the high setting is twice the size of the coefficients. Commonly available software programs will provide these coefficients as well as the grand mean. The prediction equation is stated, for two factors, as:

$$y = \text{grand mean} + \beta_1 X_1 + \beta_2 X_2 + \beta_3 (X_1 \times X_2)$$

11. Calculate the percent contribution of each factor and each interaction relative to the total "sum of the squares."

- This is also called *epsilon squared*. It is calculated by dividing the sum of the squares for each factor by the total sum of the squares and is a rough evaluation of "practical" significance.

12. Translate the mathematical model into process terms and formulate conclusions and recommendations.

13. Replicate optimum conditions and verify that results are in the predicted range. Plan the next experiment or institutionalize the change.

Example:

An organization decided that it wanted to improve yield by investigating the pressure and temperature in one of its processes. Coded values for pressure and temperature were set at -1 and +1. The design and sample size chosen involved two replications of a 2^2 design for a total of eight runs. The experiment was conducted and the results were recorded in the data sheet on the next page.

Run Order	Pressure	Temperature	Yield
1	-1	1	10
2	1	-1	15
3	-1	-1	23
4	1	-1	16
5	-1	-1	25
6	-1	1	9
7	1	1	8
8	1	1	6

The Analysis of Variance (ANOVA) table for the full model was then constructed:

Source of Variation	Sum of Squares	Degrees of Freedom	Mean Square	F_0	p-Value
Pressure (P)	60.5	1	60.50	48.4	0.002
Temperature (T)	264.5	1	264.50	211.6	0.000
Interaction (P x T)	18.0	1	18.00	18.0	0.019
Error	5.0	4	1.25		
Total	348.0	7			

The ANOVA table was reviewed to eliminate the effects with a p-value above α. Because both main effects and the interaction were below the chosen α of 0.05, all three were included in the final model. The residual plots were analyzed in three ways, to ensure that the model fit: 1) The residuals were plotted against the order of the data using an Individuals Chart and Run Chart to check that they were randomly distributed about zero. 2) A normal probability plot was run on the residuals. 3) A plot of the residuals vs. the fitted or predicted values was run to check that the variances were equal (i.e., the residuals were independent of the fitted values).

Creating an interactions plot for pressure and temperature showed that the optimum setting to maximize yield was to set both temperature and pressure at -1.

Pressure/Temperature Interactions Plot

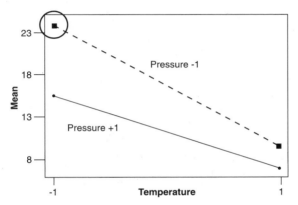

The chosen mathematical model involved the prediction equation:

$$y = \text{grand mean} + \beta_1 X_1 + \beta_2 X_2 + \beta_3(X_1 \times X_2)$$

Substituting a grand mean of 14.00 and coefficients of -2.75 for pressure, -5.75 for temperature, and 1.50 for (P x T) into the equation, we get:

$$y = 14.00 - 2.75(\text{Pressure}) - 5.75(\text{Temperature}) + 1.5(P \times T)$$

Using the optimum settings of pressure = -1 and temperature = -1 that were identified earlier forces the setting for the interaction (P x T) to be (-1) x (-1) = +1.

Substituting these values into the prediction equation, we get:

$$y = 14.00 - 2.75(-1) - 5.75(-1) + 1.5(+1) = 24.00$$

This equation tells us that, to increase yield, the pressure and temperature must be lowered. The results should be verified via confirmation runs and experiments at even lower settings of temperature and pressure should also be considered.

How do I pick factor settings?

- Process knowledge: Understand that standard operating conditions in the process could limit the range for the factors of interest. Optimum settings may be outside this range. For this reason, choose bold settings, while never forgetting safety.

- Risk: Always consider that bold settings could possibly endanger equipment or individuals and must be evaluated for such risk. Avoid settings that have the potential for harm.

- Cost: Cost is always a consideration. Time, materials, and / or resource constraints may also impact the design.

- Linearity: If there is a suspected nonlinear effect, budget for runs to explore for curvature and also make sure the inference space is large enough to detect the nonlinear effect.

Notation

The general notation to designate a fractional factorial design is:

$$2^{k-p}_R$$

$$2^{4-1}_{IV}$$ Four factors at two levels, evaluated in eight runs. Resolution is IV.

Where:

- k is the number of factors to be investigated.
- p designates the fraction of the design.
- 2^{k-p} is the number of runs. For example, a 2^5 design requires thirty-two runs, a 2^{5-1} (or 2^4) design requires sixteen runs (a half-fractional design), and a 2^{5-2} (or 2^3) design requires eight runs (a quarter-fractional design).
- R is the resolution.

How does coding work?

Coding is the representation of the settings picked in standardized format. Coding allows for clear comparison of the effects of the chosen factors.

The design matrix for 2^k factorials is usually shown in standard order. The Yates standard order has the first factor alternate low settings, then high settings, throughout the runs. The second factor in the design alternates two runs at the low setting, followed by two runs at the high setting.

The low level of a factor is designated with a "-" or -1 and the high level is designated with a "+" or 1. An example of a design matrix for a 2^2 factorial appears on the next page.

A 2^2 and 2^3 Factorial Design Matrix

Temperature	Concentration
-1	-1
1	-1
-1	1
1	1

Adding another factor duplicates the design.

Factor	Level Low	High
Temperature (A)	-1	1
Concentration (B)	-1	1
Catalyst (C)	-1	1

Temperature	Concentration	Catalyst
-1	-1	-1
1	-1	-1
-1	1	-1
1	1	-1
-1	-1	1
1	-1	1
-1	1	1
1	1	1

Tip It is easy to increase the factors in a full factorial design by doubling the previous model and making the first-half settings low and the second-half settings high for the added factor.

Coded values can be analyzed using the ANOVA method and yield a $y = f(x)$ prediction equation.

Tip The prediction equation will be different for coded vs. uncoded units. However, the output range will be the same.

Even though the actual factor settings in an example might be temperature 160° and 180° C, 20% and 40% concentration, and catalysts A and B, all the settings could be analyzed using -1 and +1 settings without losing any validity.

How do I choose fractional vs. full DOEs?

There are advantages and disadvantages for all DOEs. The DOE chosen for a particular situation will depend on the conditions involved.

Advantages of full factorial DOEs:

- All possible combinations can be covered.
- Analysis is straightforward, as there is no aliasing.

Disadvantages of full factorial DOEs:

- The cost of the experiment increases as the number of factors increases. For instance, in a two-factor two-level experiment (2^2), four runs are needed to cover the effect of A, B, AB, and the grand mean. In a five-factor two-level experiment (2^5), thirty-two runs are required to do a full factorial. Many of these runs are used to evaluate higher order interactions that the Black Belt may not be interested in. In a 2^5 experiment, there are five one-way effects (A,B,C,D,E), ten two-ways, ten three-ways, five four-ways, and one five-way effect. The 2^2 experiment has 75% of its runs spent learning about the likely one-way and two-way effects, while the 2^5 design only spends less than 50% of its runs examining these one-way and two-way effects.

Advantages of fractional factorial DOEs:

- Less money and effort is spent for the same amount of data.
- It takes less time to do fewer experiments.
- If data analysis indicates, runs can be added to eliminate confounding.

Disadvantages of fractional factorial DOEs:

- Analysis of higher order interactions could be complex.
- Confounding could mask factor and interaction effects.

How do I set up a fractional factorial DOE?

The effect of confounding should be minimized when setting up a fractional factorial. The Yates standard order will show the level settings of each factor and a coded value for all the interactions. For example, when A is high (+1) and B is low (-1), the interaction factor AB is (+1 x -1 = -1).

A column for each interaction can thus be constructed as shown here:

Level Settings and Interactions

						Factor D
A	B	C	A x B	A x C	B x C	A x B x C
-1	-1	-1	1	1	1	-1
1	-1	-1	-1	-1	1	1
-1	1	-1	-1	1	-1	1
1	1	-1	1	-1	-1	-1
-1	-1	1	1	-1	-1	1
1	-1	1	-1	1	-1	-1
-1	1	1	-1	-1	1	-1
1	1	1	1	1	1	1

Running a full factorial experiment with one more factor (D) would require a doubling of the number of runs. If factor D settings are substituted for a likely insignificant effect, that expense can be saved. The highest interaction is the least likely candidate to have a significant effect.

In this case, replacing the A x B x C interaction with factor D allows the Black Belt to say ABC was aliased or confounded with D.

(**Note**: The three-level interaction still exists, but will be confounded with the factor D. All credit for any output change will be attributed to factor D. This is a direct application of the sparsity of effects principle.)

In fact there is more aliasing than just D and ABC. Aliasing two-way and three-way effects can also be accomplished and can be computed in two ways:

1. By multiplying any two columns together (such as column A and column D), each of the values in the new column (AD) will be either -1 or +1. If the resulting column matches any other (in this case, it will match column BC), those two effects can be said to be confounded.

2. The Identity value (I) can be discovered and multiplied to get the aliased values. For example, in this case, because D=ABC (also called the design generator), the Identity value is ABCD. Multiplying this Identity value by a factor will calculate its aliases. Multiplying ABCD and D will equal ABCDD. Because any column multiplied by itself will create a column of 1's (multiplication identity), the D^2 term drops out, leaving ABC and reaffirming that D=ABC. The entire aliasing structure for this example is shown on the next page.

Aliasing Structure

Runs: 8 Fraction: 1/2
Design Generators: D = ABC
Alias Structure
I + ABCD

A + BCD	AB + CD
B + ACD	AC + BD
C + ABD	AD + BC
D + ABC	

What fractional factorials are available?

Adding an additional factor to a full factorial without adding any additional runs will create a half fractional design. (The design has half the runs needed for a full factorial. If a design has one-quarter the runs needed for full factorial analysis, it is a quarter fractional design, etc.) The key to selecting the type of run and number of factors is to understand what the resolution of the design is, for any given number of factors and available runs. The Black Belt must decide how much confounding he or she is willing to accept. A partial list of fractional designs is included below.

Number of Factors	Number of Runs	Fraction	Resolution
3	4	Half	III
4	8	Half	IV
5	8	Quarter	III
5	16	Half	V
6	8	Eighth	III
6	16	Quarter	IV
6	32	Half	VI

DOE Variations

What is Response Surface Method?

The Response Surface Method (RSM) is a technique that enables the Black Belt to find the optimum condition for a response (y) given two or more significant factors (x's).

For the case of two factors, the basic strategy is to consider the graphical representation of the yield as a function of the two significant factors. The RSM graphic is similar to the contours of a topographical map. The higher up the "hill," the better the yield. Data is gathered to enable the contours of the map to be plotted. Once done, the resulting map is used to find the path of steepest ascent to the maximum or steepest descent to the minimum. The ultimate RSM objective is to determine the optimum operating conditions for the system or to determine a region of the factor space in which the operating specifications are satisfied (usually using a second-order model).

RSM terms:

- The *response surface* is the surface represented by the expected value of an output modeled as a function of significant inputs (variable inputs only):

$$\text{Expected (y)} = f(x_1, x_2, x_3, \ldots x_n)$$

- The *method of steepest ascent* or *descent* is a procedure for moving sequentially along the direction of the maximum increase (steepest ascent) or maximum decrease (steepest descent) of the response variable using the first-order model:

$$\text{y (predicted)} = \beta_0 + \Sigma \, \beta_i \, x_i$$

- The *region of curvature* is the region where one or more of the significant inputs will no longer conform to the first-order model. Once in this region of operation, most responses can be modeled using the following fitted second-order model:

y (predicted) = $\beta_0 + \Sigma \beta_i x_i + \Sigma \beta_{ii} x_i x_{i\,+} + \Sigma \beta_{ij} x_i x_j$

- The *central composite design* is a common DOE matrix used to establish a valid second-order model.

How do I do it?

1. Select the y. Select the associated confirmed x's and boldly select their experimental ranges.

   - These x's should have been confirmed to have a significant effect on the y through prior experimentation.

2. Add center points to the basic 2^{k-p} design.

   - A center point is a point halfway between the high and low settings of each factor.

3. Conduct the DOE and plot the resulting data on a response surface.

4. Determine the direction of steepest ascent to an optimum y.

5. Reset the x values to move the DOE in the direction of the optimum y.

   - In general, the next DOE should have x values that overlap those used in the previous experiment.

6. Continue to conduct DOEs, evaluate the results, and step in the direction of the optimal y until a constraint has been encountered or the data shows that the optimum has been reached.

An Example RSM Graphic

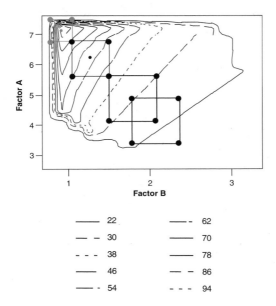

—— 22		——-· 62	
— — 30		—— 70	
- - - 38		—— 78	
—— 46		— — 86	
——-· 54		- - - 94	

7. **Add additional points to the last design to create a central composite design to allow for a second-order evaluation. (The central composite design is described later in this chapter.)**

   • This will verify if the analysis is at a maximum or minimum condition. If the condition is at an optimum solution, then the process is ended. If the second-order evaluation shows that the condition is not yet at optimum, it will provide direction for the next sequential experiment.

An illustration of a central composite design for two factors is shown below.

Central Composite Design

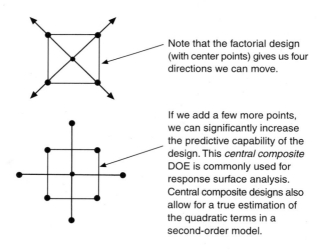

Note that the factorial design (with center points) gives us four directions we can move.

If we add a few more points, we can significantly increase the predictive capability of the design. This *central composite* DOE is commonly used for response surface analysis. Central composite designs also allow for a true estimation of the quadratic terms in a second-order model.

RSM is intended to be a sequence of experiments with an attempt to "dial in to an optimum setting." Whenever an apparent optimum is reached, additional points are added to perform a more rigorous second-order evaluation.

What is a Box-Behnken design?

A Box-Behnken design looks like a basic factorial design with a center point, except that the corner points are missing and replaced with points on the edges. This type of design is used when the corner point settings are impossible or impractical because of their combined severity. Running three factors at their high settings could produce a volatile situation.

Advantages:

- It is more efficient than three-level full factorials.
- It is excellent for trials where corner points are not recommended.
- It allows all two-factor interactions to be modeled.
- It can identify interactions and quadratic effects.

Disadvantages:

- Enough trials must be run to estimate all one-way and two-way effects (even if only one-way effects are of interest).
- It is hard to modify into other studies.

What is a Box-Wilson (central composite) design?

A Box-Wilson design is a rotatable design (subject to number of blocks) that allows for the identification of nonlinear effects. Rotatability is the characteristic that ensures constant prediction variance at all points equidistant from the design center and thus improves the quality of prediction. The design consists of a cube portion made up from the characteristics of 2^k factorial designs or 2^{k-n} fractional factorial designs, axial points, and center points.

Box-Wilson Design

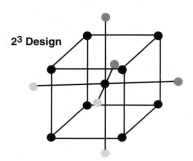

2³ Design

Factor A	Factor B	Factor C
-1	-1	-1
1	-1	-1
-1	1	-1
1	1	-1
-1	-1	1
1	-1	1
-1	1	1
1	1	1
-1.68179	0	0
1.68179	0	0
0	-1.68179	0
0	1.68179	0
0	0	-1.68179
0	0	1.68179
0	0	0
0	0	0
0	0	0
0	0	0
0	0	0
0	0	0

Advantages:

- It is a highly efficient second-order modeling design for quantitative factors.

- It can be created by adding additional points to a 2^{k-p} design, provided the original design was at least Resolution V or higher.

Disadvantages:

- It does not work with qualitative factors.
- Axial points may exceed the settings of the simple model and may be outside the ability of the process to produce.

What is a Plackett-Burman design?

Plackett-Burman designs are orthogonal designs of Resolution III that are primarily used for screening designs. Each two-way interaction is positively or negatively aliased with a main effect.

Advantages:

- A limited number of runs are needed to evaluate a lot of factors.
- Clever assignment of factors might allow the Black Belt to determine which factor caused the output, despite aliasing.

Disadvantages:

- It assumes the interactions are not strong enough to mask the main effects.
- Aliasing can be complex.

What are EVOP and PLEX designs?

Evolutionary operation (EVOP) is a continuous improvement design. Plant experimentation (PLEX) is a sequence of corrective designs meant to obtain rapid improvement. Both designs are typically small full factorial designs with possible center points. They are designed to be run while maintaining production; therefore, the inference space is typically very small.

Advantages:

- They do not disrupt production and can be used in an administrative situation.

- They force the organization to investigate factor relationships and prove factory physics.

Disadvantages:

- They can be time-consuming. For example, because, in PLEX, levels are generally set conservatively to ensure that production is not degraded, it is sometimes difficult to prove statistical validity with a single design. A first design may be used to simply decide factor levels for a subsequent design.

- They require continuous and significant management support.

What are Taguchi designs?

Taguchi designs are orthogonal designs that have, as a primary goal, finding factor settings that minimize response variation, while adjusting the process (or keeping it on target). This is called robust parameter design. The solution will reduce variation of the process and/or reduce sensitivity to noise. (Details of Taguchi designs are beyond the scope of this book. For more detailed information, see *Design of Experiments Using the Taguchi Approach: 16 Steps to Product and Process Improvement* by Ranjit K. Roy.)

Failure Mode and Effects Analysis

Why use it?

Failure Mode and Effects Analysis (FMEA) allows an assessment of the risk to customers if a key process input (x) were to fail. The FMEA also helps to determine what actions to take to minimize this risk. (The customer could be the end user of a product or a downstream operation in an organization.) FMEAs are also used to document processes and process improvement activities.

Note: There are a number of different FMEAs including design, systems, product, and process FMEAs. This chapter describes process FMEAs.

What does it do?

The FMEA provides a documented summary of the team's thoughts regarding risk to the customer if any of the key process inputs to the process fails. Furthermore, the FMEA contains the recommended and implemented actions to minimize this risk. It is a living document that must be reviewed and updated whenever the process has been modified.

Initially, the FMEA is completed in the Measure phase of DMAIC and can provide recommended actions for the team to minimize risk to the customer. Revisions to the FMEA continue into the Analyze and Improve phases to ensure that the evaluation criteria (severity, occurrence, and detection) and cause/effect relationships are updated with data-driven conclusions. During the Control phase, the FMEA needs to be updated to reflect the final state of the improved project. The information from the FMEA will then be summarized in the control plan document and given to the process owner.

How do I do it?

The initial information needed for an FMEA is a list of Key Process Input Variables (x's). This list of x's can come from process maps, a Cause and Effect Matrix, a Cause & Effect Diagram/brainstorming session, or existing process data.

The following figure shows a typical process FMEA form. The description that follows is the method used to complete this form. (The numbers correspond to the numbers in the graphic.)

A Typical FMEA Form

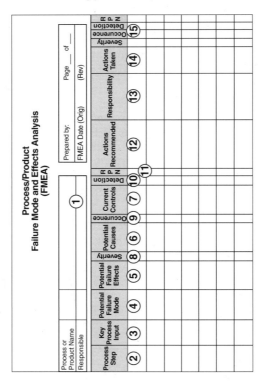

1. Include information to identify who completed the form, when the form was completed, and what process the form represents.

2. List the process step from which the key process input (x) is controlled.

3. List the specific key process input (x) of interest.

4. List the potential failure modes for this key process input. (**Note**: There may be more than one failure mode.) Describe the failure mode(s) in physical or technical terms, not as a symptom (effect) noted by the customer.

5. If the key process input (x) fails, list the effect that the customer experiences. For example, if a fitting on a brake hose was not properly adjusted, the customer would experience "loss of brake pressure."

6. List the potential cause(s) for this failure mode. There may be more than one cause per failure mode. Also consider operating conditions, usage or in-service, and possible combinations as potential causes.

7. List the controls that are currently in place to detect the cause of the failure mode.

8. On a scale from 1-10, rate the severity of the failure effect the customer experiences.

9. On a scale from 1-10, determine how often the cause of the failure mode occurs.

10. On a scale from 1-10, determine how effective the current controls can detect the cause of the failure mode. If a good detection system (such as an automated feedback system) is in place, assign a 1 or 2 to this column. If no controls are in place, assign a 10 to this column.

Note: A typical ranking system for steps 8, 9, and 10 is shown in the following figure:

FMEA Rankings

Rating	Severity	Occurrence	Detection
High 10	Hazardous without warning	Very high and almost inevitable	Cannot detect, or detection with very low probability
	Loss of primary function	High repeated failures	Remote or low chance of detection
	Loss of secondary function	Moderate failures	Low detection probability
	Minor defect	Occasional failures	Moderate detection probability
Low 1	No effect	Failure unlikely	Almost certain detection

11. Multiply the severity, occurrence, and detection ratings together to calculate a risk priority number (RPN). The highest possible RPN would be 1000 and the lowest RPN would be 1. Low values indicate lower risk. The RPN is one indicator as to which key process inputs (x) recommended actions should be identified for, to reduce risk to the customer (step 12). If, however, any key process inputs (x) have a severity rating of 9 or 10, efforts should first focus on these key process inputs to ensure detection is at least a 1 or 2 and occurrence is also a low number.

12. Use the RPN to determine and discuss what recommended action will be taken to minimize risk to the customer.

    Note: Recommended actions can only impact detection or occurrence. The severity cannot change unless the product, service, or information is used for a different intent. If a high severity rating is observed, consider speaking to the process designers to determine if this key process input can be designed out of the process.

13. Identify the person responsible for completing the recommended action. Include the person's name, not his or her job function, as well as the anticipated completion date.

14. After the assigned person has completed the recommended actions, list the specific actions taken, along with the actual completion date.

15. Based on the completed actions, reevaluate the severity, occurrence, and detection to calculate a new risk priority number.

Current controls from the FMEA should be noted in the initial control plan. The FMEA needs to be updated after the project is completed but prior to handing off to the process owner, to reflect the completed project. The final FMEA will be used to finalize the control plan. If, in the future, changes are made to the process, the FMEA will need to be reviewed and updated.

Example:

A Black Belt working for a national travel agency was interested in determining why there were large discrepancies between the booked cost of airline tickets and computer-generated "lowest cost fares." These cost overruns had to be resolved to maintain one of the agency's largest corporate clients. Having performed a Cause and Effect Matrix on the process, the Black Belt narrowed his focus to five process steps thought to be highly correlated with the customer requirement of "lowest cost fares." ("SNAP" is the name of a button on the travel agency's Sabre computer system.) A segment of the detailed process map being evaluated is shown on the following page.

Travel Agency Process Map

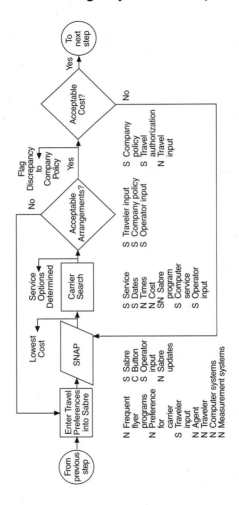

Shown in the following figure is a portion of the completed FMEA.

The Travel Agency FMEA

Process Step	Key Process Input	Potential Failure Mode	Potential Failure Effects	Severity	Potential Causes	Occurrence	Current Controls	Detection	R P N	Actions Recommended	Responsibility	Actions Taken	Severity	Occurrence	Detection	R P N
Travel Prefs.	Pref. for Freq. Flyer Prog.	Lowest cost fare rejected by traveler	Flight not booked at lowest cost fare	10	Traveler override at low cost fare for frequent flyer	6	Comp. pol. restrictions and agent familiarity with policy	4	240	Data collection plan to determine number of defects for this cause	BB to create a plan for team review by Friday					0
Travel Prefs.	Traveler pref. for carrier	Lowest cost fare rejected by traveler	Flight not booked at lowest cost fare	10	Traveler pref. for carrier	4	Comp. pol. restrictions and agent familiarity with policy	4	160	Data collection plan to determine number of defects for this cause	BB to create a plan for team review by Friday					0
SNAP	Sabre-system operator input	SNAP not activated to search for lowest fare	Flight not booked at lowest cost fare	10	Agent forgot to SNAP	5	None; SNAP is only a push of the button but not regulated/detected as part of standard operations	10	500	Data collection plan to determine number of transactions that are not SNAP'ed; Mistake-proof system so that SNAP is automatic	BB to create a plan for team review by Friday	Data collection; Use of SNAP is not consistent between operators; Fairly consistent within operator; Automated the SNAP function	10	1	1	10

Continued on the next page

Process		Potential Failure Mode	Potential Failure Effects	SEV	Potential Causes	OCC	Current Controls	DET	RPN	Recommended Actions	Responsibility				
SNAP	Sabre-system operator input	Agent unable to use SNAP function (disabled)	Flight not booked at lowest cost fare	10	Sabre system down	2	Agency at mercy of Sabre system; No control; over Sabre system up/down time	10	200	Determine % system downtime and times of occurrence	BB and JC; Sabre point of contact for agency				0
Accept Cost	Comp. Policy	Comp. policy not adhered to	Flight not booked at lowest cost fare	10	Agent not informed/ trained on client company policy/restrictions	5	Agents receive 8 weeks of training at hire; Policy books intended for update within request	8	400	Provide updates policies and refresher training; enable electronic capture of red-flags	SA & AK to eval. updates & training; IT for ability				0
Accept Cost	Comp. Policy	Old policy followed	Traveler override not placed on red-flag report to client billing	7	Policy not updated; Operator does not flag	4	Policies are supposed to be updated within 7 days of client request	10	280	Provide updates to policies and refresher training; One source on web	SA & AK to eval. updates & training; IT for ability				0

Results of the FMEA and a list of prioritized actions were summarized using a Pareto Chart, as shown in the following figure:

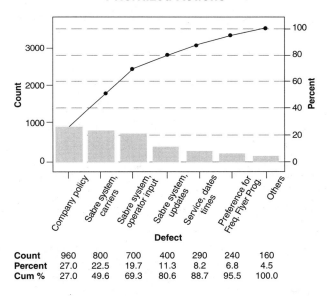

Prioritized Actions

	Company policy	Sabre system, carriers	Sabre system, operator input	Sabre system, updates	Service, dates times	Preference for Freq. Flyer Prog.	Others
Count	960	800	700	400	290	240	160
Percent	27.0	22.5	19.7	11.3	8.2	6.8	4.5
Cum %	27.0	49.6	69.3	80.6	88.7	95.5	100.0

The Pareto Chart of the FMEA RPNs indicates which process inputs are the potential Key Process Input Variables that exhibit the greatest leverage on the cost of fares. The category with the highest RPN would be the best place for the Black Belt to focus on.

The Black Belt also categorized the inputs into related causes and created a Pareto Chart to sum the results, as shown on the next page.

Cause Categories

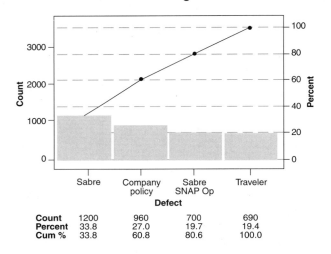

	Sabre	Company policy	Sabre SNAP Op	Traveler
Count	1200	960	700	690
Percent	33.8	27.0	19.7	19.4
Cum %	33.8	60.8	80.6	100.0

The Black Belt recognized that most of the Sabre-related issues were out of the team's control.

The FMEA indicated that the Black Belt needed to create a data collection plan to validate assumptions in remaining areas. The FMEA would need to be updated as progress on the project continued.

 **Control Charts**

Why use it?

Control Charts are used to monitor, control, and improve process performance over time by studying variation and its source.

What does it do?

A Control Chart:

- Focuses attention on detecting and monitoring process variation over time.

- Distinguishes special from common causes of variation, as a guide to local or management action.

- Serves as a tool for ongoing control of a process.

- Helps improve a process to perform consistently and predictably for higher quality, lower cost, and higher effective capacity.

- Provides a common language for discussing process performance.

How do I do it?

There are many types of Control Charts. The Control Chart(s) that a team decides to use will be determined by the type of data it has. The Tree Diagram on the next page will help to determine which Control Chart(s) will best fit each particular situation.

Choose the appropriate Control Chart based on the type of data and sample size.

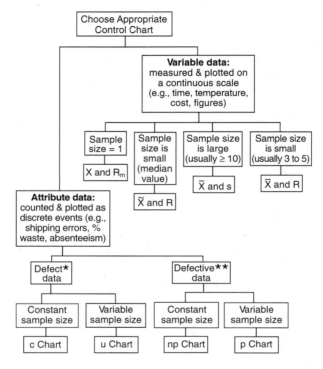

* A *defect* is a failure to meet one of the acceptance criteria. A defective unit might have multiple defects.

** *Defective* is when an entire unit fails to meet acceptance criteria, regardless of the number of defects on the unit.

Constructing Control Charts

1. **Select the process to be charted.**

2. **Determine the sampling method and plan.**

    - To determine how large a sample can be drawn, balance the time and cost to collect a sample with the amount of information that will be gathered. For attribute charts the suggested sample size is at least fifty, and for variable data charts a suggested minimum is three to five. For a c or u chart, the sample needs to be large enough to average five or more defects per lot.

    - As much as possible, obtain the samples under the same technical conditions: the same machine, operator, lot, and so on.

    - Frequency of sampling will depend on an ability to discern patterns in the data. Consider hourly, daily, shifts, monthly, annually, lots, and so on. Once the process is "in control," consider reducing the frequency with which samples are chosen.

    - Generally, collect 20–25 groups of samples before calculating the statistics and control limits.

    Tip Make sure samples are random. To establish the inherent variation of a process, allow the process to run untouched (i.e., according to standard procedures).

3. **Initiate data collection.**

    - Run the process untouched and gather sampled data.

    - Record data on an appropriate Control Chart sheet or other graph paper. Include any unusual events that occur.

4. Calculate the appropriate statistics.

a) If attribute data was collected, use the Attribute Data Table, Central Line column.

Attribute Data Table

Type Control Chart	Sample Size	Central Line	Control Limits
Fraction defective	Variable (usually ≥ 50)	For each subgroup: $p = np/n$	$^*UCL_p = \bar{p} + 3\sqrt{\dfrac{\bar{p}(1-\bar{p})}{n}}$
p Chart		For all subgroups: $\bar{p} = \Sigma np/\Sigma n$	$^*LCL_p = \bar{p} - 3\sqrt{\dfrac{\bar{p}(1-\bar{p})}{n}}$
Number defective	Constant (usually ≥ 50)	For each subgroup: $np = \#$ defective units	$UCL_{np} = n\bar{p} + 3\sqrt{n\bar{p}(1-\bar{p})}$
np Chart		For all subgroups: $n\bar{p} = \Sigma np/k$	$LCL_{np} = n\bar{p} - 3\sqrt{n\bar{p}(1-\bar{p})}$
Number of defects	Constant	For each subgroup: $c = \#$ defects	$UCL_c = \bar{c} + 3\sqrt{\bar{c}}$
c Chart		For all subgroups: $\bar{c} = \Sigma c/k$	$LCL_c = \bar{c} - 3\sqrt{\bar{c}}$
Number of defects per unit	Variable	For each subgroup: $u = c/n$	$^*UCL_u = \bar{u} + 3\sqrt{\dfrac{\bar{u}}{n}}$
u Chart		For all subgroups: $\bar{u} = \Sigma c/\Sigma n$	$^*LCL_u = \bar{u} - 3\sqrt{\dfrac{\bar{u}}{n}}$

$np = \#$ defective units
$c = \#$ of defects
$n =$ sample size within each subgroup
$k = \#$ of subgroups

* This formula creates changing control limits. To avoid this, use average sample sizes $\bar{n}$ for those samples that are within $\pm 20\%$ of the average sample size. Calculate individual limits for the samples exceeding $\pm 20\%$.

b) If variable data was collected, use the Variable Data Table, Central Line column.

Variable Data Table

Type Control Chart	Sample Size n	Central Line*	Control Limits
Average & Range	<10, but usually 3 to 5	$\bar{\bar{X}} = \dfrac{(\bar{X}_1 + \bar{X}_2 + \dots \bar{X}_k)}{k}$	$UCL_{\bar{x}} = \bar{\bar{X}} + A_2\bar{R}$ $LCL_{\bar{x}} = \bar{\bar{X}} - A_2\bar{R}$
$\bar{X}$ and R		$\bar{R} = \dfrac{(R_1 + R_2 + \dots R_k)}{k}$	$UCL_R = D_4\bar{R}$ $LCL_R = D_3\bar{R}$
Average & Standard Deviation	Usually ≥ 10	$\bar{\bar{X}} = \dfrac{(\bar{X}_1 + \bar{X}_2 + \dots \bar{X}_k)}{k}$	$UCL_{\bar{x}} = \bar{\bar{X}} + A_3\bar{s}$ $LCL_{\bar{x}} = \bar{\bar{X}} - A_3\bar{s}$
$\bar{X}$ and s		$\bar{s} = \dfrac{(s_1 + s_2 + \dots s_k)}{k}$	$UCL_s = B_4\bar{s}$ $LCL_s = B_3\bar{s}$
Median & Range	<10, but usually 3 or 5	$\bar{\bar{\tilde{X}}} = \dfrac{(\tilde{X}_1 + \tilde{X}_2 + \dots \tilde{X}_k)}{k}$	$UCL_{\tilde{x}} = \bar{\bar{X}} + \tilde{A}_2\bar{R}$ $LCL_{\tilde{x}} = \bar{\bar{X}} - \tilde{A}_2\bar{R}$
$\tilde{X}$ and R		$\bar{R} = \dfrac{(R_1 + R_2 + \dots R_k)}{k}$	$UCL_R = D_4\bar{R}$ $LCL_R = D_3\bar{R}$
Individuals & Moving Range	1	$\bar{X} = \dfrac{(X_1 + X_2 + \dots X_k)}{k}$	$UCL_X = \bar{X} + E_2\bar{R}_m$ $LCL_X = \bar{X} - E_2\bar{R}_m$
X and R_m		$R_m = |(X_{i+1} - X_i)|$ $\bar{R}_m = \dfrac{(R_1 + R_2 + \dots R_{k-1})}{k-1}$	$UCL_{Rm} = D_4\bar{R}_m$ $LCL_{Rm} = D_3\bar{R}_m$

k = # of subgroups, $\tilde{X}$ = median value within each subgroup
* For constant size subgroups only

5. Calculate the control limits.

a) For attribute data, use the Attribute Data Table, Control Limits column.

b) For variable data, use the Variable Data Table, Control Limits column for the correct formula to use.

- Use the Table of Constants (on the next page) to match the numeric values to the constants in the formulas shown in the Control Limits column of the Variable Data Table. The values to look up will depend on the type of Variable Control Chart chosen and on the size of the sample drawn.

Tip If the Lower Control Limit (LCL) of an Attribute Data Control Chart is a negative number, set the LCL to zero.

Tip The p and u formulas create changing control limits if the sample sizes vary subgroup to subgroup. To avoid this, use the average sample size n for those samples that are within ±20% of the average sample size. Calculate individual limits for the samples exceeding ±20%.

6. Construct the Control Chart(s).

- For Attribute Data Control Charts, construct one chart, plotting each subgroup's proportion or number defective, number of defects, or defects per unit.

- For Variable Data Control Charts, construct two charts: on the top chart, plot each subgroup's mean, median, or individuals, and on the bottom chart, plot each subgroup's range or standard deviation.

©2002 GOAL/QPC,
Six Sigma Academy

Table of Constants

Sample Size n	$\bar{X}$ and R Chart			$\bar{X}$ and s Chart			
	A_2	D_3	D_4	A_3	B_3	B_4	c_4^*
2	1.880	0	3.267	2.659	0	3.267	.7979
3	1.023	0	2.574	1.954	0	2.568	.8862
4	0.729	0	2.282	1.628	0	2.266	.9213
5	0.577	0	2.114	1.427	0	2.089	.9400
6	0.483	0	2.004	1.287	0.030	1.970	.9515
7	0.419	0.076	1.924	1.182	0.118	1.882	.9594
8	0.373	0.136	1.864	1.099	0.185	1.815	.9650
9	0.337	0.184	1.816	1.032	0.239	1.761	.9693
10	0.308	0.223	1.777	0.975	0.284	1.716	.9727

Sample Size n	$\tilde{X}$ and R Chart			X and R_m Chart			
	$\tilde{A}_2$	D_3	D_4	E_2	D_3	D_4	d_2^*
2	- - - -	0	3.267	2.659	0	3.267	1.128
3	1.187	0	2.574	1.772	0	2.574	1.693
4	- - - -	0	2.282	1.457	0	2.282	2.059
5	0.691	0	2.114	1.290	0	2.114	2.326
6	- - - -	0	2.004	1.184	0	2.004	2.534
7	0.509	0.076	1.924	1.109	0.076	1.924	2.704
8	- - - -	0.136	1.864	1.054	0.136	1.864	2.847
9	0.412	0.184	1.816	1.010	0.184	1.816	2.970
10	- - - -	0.223	1.777	0.975	0.223	1.777	3.078

* Useful in estimating the process standard deviation $\hat{\sigma}$.

Note: The minimum sample size shown in this chart is 2 because variation in the form of a range can only be calculated in samples greater than 1. The X and R_m Chart creates these minimum samples by combining and then calculating the difference between sequential, individual measurements.

- Draw a solid horizontal line on each chart. This line corresponds to the process average.

- Draw dashed lines for the upper and lower control limits.

Interpreting Control Charts

- *Attribute Data Control Charts* are based on one chart. The charts for fraction or number defective, number of defects, or number of defects per unit, measure variation *between samples*. *Variable Data Control Charts* are based on two charts: the one on top, for averages, medians, and individuals, measures variation *between subgroups* over time; the chart below, for ranges and standard deviations, measures variation *within subgroups* over time.

- Determine if the process mean (center line) is where it should be relative to customer specifications or internal business needs or objectives. If not, then it is an indication that something has changed in the process, the customer requirements or objectives have changed, or the process has never been centered.

- Analyze the data relative to the control limits; distinguish between *common* causes and *special* causes. The fluctuation of the points within the limits results from variation inherent in the process. This variation results from common causes within the system (e.g., design, choice of machine, preventive maintenance) and can only be affected by changing that system. However, points outside of the limits or patterns within the limits come from a special cause (e.g., human errors, unplanned events, freak occurrences) that is not part of the way the process normally operates, or is present because of an unlikely

©2002 GOAL/QPC,
Six Sigma Academy

combination of process steps. Special causes must be eliminated before the Control Chart can be used as a monitoring tool. Once this is done, the process will be "in control" and samples can be taken at regular intervals to make sure that the process doesn't fundamentally change. (See the "Determining if the Process is Out of Control" section of this chapter.)

- A process is in "statistical control" if the process is not being affected by special causes (the influence of an individual or machine). All the points must fall within the control limits and they must be randomly dispersed about the average line for an in-control system.

Tip "Control" doesn't necessarily mean that the product or service will meet the needs. It only means that the process is *consistent.* Don't confuse control limits with specification limits— specification limits are related to customer requirements, not process variation.

Tip Any points outside the control limits, once identified with a cause (or causes), should be removed and the calculations and charts redone. Points within the control limits, but showing indications of trends, shifts, or instability, are also special causes.

Tip When a Control Chart has been initiated and all special causes removed, continue to plot new data on a new chart, but DO NOT recalculate the control limits. As long as the process does not change, the limits should not be changed. Control limits should be recalculated only when a permanent, desired change has occurred in the process, and only using data *after* the change occurred.

Tip Nothing will change just because a chart was created! An action must occur. Form a team to investigate. (See the "Common Questions for Investigating an Out-of-Control Process" list in this chapter.)

Determining if the Process is Out of Control

A process is said to be "out of control" if either one of these is true:

1.   One or more points fall outside of the control limits.*

2.   When the Control Chart is divided into zones, as shown below, any of the following points are true:

- - - - - - - - - -	Upper Control Limit
Zone A	(UCL)
Zone B	
Zone C	
	Average
Zone C	
Zone B	
Zone A	Lower Control Limit
- - - - - - - - - -	(LCL)

a) Two points, out of three consecutive points, are on the same side of the average in Zone A or beyond.

b) Four points, out of five consecutive points, are on the same side of the average in Zone B or beyond.

c) Nine consecutive points are on one side of the average.

d) There are six consecutive points, increasing or decreasing.*

e) There are fourteen consecutive points that alternate up and down.*

f) There are fifteen consecutive points within Zone C (above and below the average).

* Applies for both variable and attribute data

©2002 GOAL/QPC,
Six Sigma Academy

Tests for Control

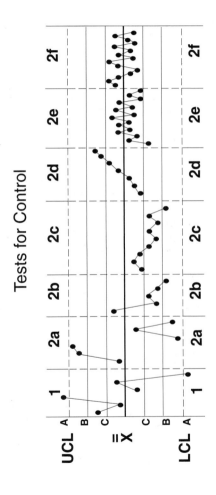

Source: Lloyd S. Nelson, Director of Statistical Methods, Nashua Corporation, New Hampshire

Common Questions for Investigating an Out-of-Control Process

❐ Yes ❐ No Are there differences in the measurement accuracy of instruments/ methods used?

❐ Yes ❐ No Are there differences in the methods used by different personnel?

❐ Yes ❐ No Is the process affected by the environment (e.g., temperature, humidity)?

❐ Yes ❐ No Has there been a significant change in the environment?

❐ Yes ❐ No Is the process affected by predictable conditions (e.g., tool wear)?

❐ Yes ❐ No Were any untrained personnel involved in the process at the time?

❐ Yes ❐ No Has there been a change in the source for input to the process (e.g., raw materials, information)?

❐ Yes ❐ No Is the process affected by employee fatigue?

❐ Yes ❐ No Has there been a change in policies or procedures (e.g., maintenance procedures)?

❐ Yes ❐ No Is the process adjusted frequently?

❐ Yes ❐ No Did the samples come from different parts of the process? Shifts? Individuals?

❐ Yes ❐ No Are employees afraid to report "bad news"?

A team should address each "Yes" answer as a potential source of a special cause.

Individuals & Moving Range Chart

IV Lines Connection Time

Process/Operation:	IV Lines Connection Open Heart Admissions		Department: Intensive Care	
Characteristic: Time in seconds	**Sample Size:** One	**Sample Frequency:** Each patient	**By:** EW	**Date:** 6/10
Individuals: k = 26	$\sum X = 8470$	$\bar{X} = 325.77$ **UCL = 645**		**LCL = 7**
Ranges: n = 2	$\sum R = 2990$	$\bar{R} = 119.6$ **UCL = 392**		**LCL = 0**

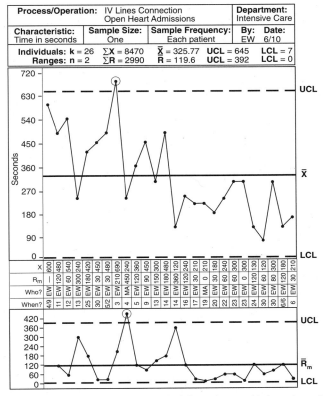

Information provided courtesy of Parkview Episcopal Medical Center

Note: Something in the process changed, and now it takes less time to make IV connections for patients being admitted for open heart surgery.

p Chart

General Dentistry: Percent of
Patients Who Failed to Keep Appointments

Historical Statistics:
$\bar{p}$ = 39   UCL = 47   LCL = 31

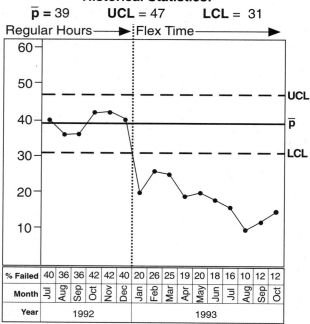

*Information provided courtesy of U.S. Navy,
Naval Dental Center, San Diego*

Note: Providing flex time for patients resulted in fewer appointments missed.

u Chart

Shop Process Check
Solder Defects

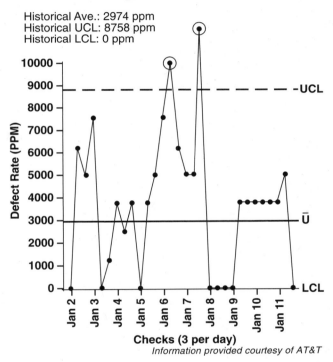

Historical Ave.: 2974 ppm
Historical UCL: 8758 ppm
Historical LCL: 0 ppm

Defect Rate (PPM)

10000
9000 ----- -UCL
8000
7000
6000
5000
4000
3000 —Ū
2000
1000
0 - LCL

Jan 2 Jan 3 Jan 4 Jan 5 Jan 6 Jan 7 Jan 8 Jan 9 Jan 10 Jan 11

Checks (3 per day)
Information provided courtesy of AT&T

X̄ & R Chart

n = 10 parts randomly sampled each hour

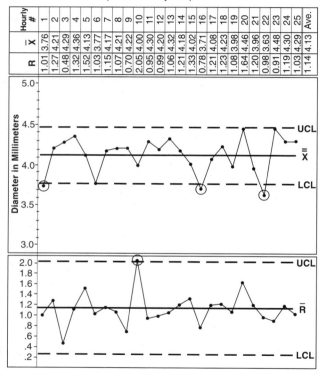

Hourly #	X̄	R
1	3.76	1.01
2	4.21	1.27
3	4.29	0.48
4	4.36	1.32
5	4.13	1.52
6	3.77	1.03
7	4.17	1.15
8	4.21	1.07
9	4.22	0.70
10	4.00	2.05
11	4.30	0.95
12	4.20	0.99
13	4.32	1.06
14	4.18	1.21
15	4.02	1.33
16	3.71	0.78
17	4.08	1.21
18	4.23	1.23
19	3.98	1.08
20	4.46	1.64
21	3.96	1.20
22	3.63	0.98
23	4.48	0.91
24	4.30	1.19
25	4.29	1.03
Ave.	4.13	1.14

*Information provided courtesy of BlueFire Partners, Inc.
and Hamilton Standard*

Note: Hours 1, 16 and 22 should be reviewed to understand why these sample averages are outside the control limts

Total Productive Maintenance and Preventative Maintenance

Why use it?

Total Productive Maintenance (TPM) is a program to continuously improve equipment operation through maintenance performed by both operators and maintenance personnel. These improvements to equipment maintainability are developed and implemented through small group activities.

The goals of TPM are:

- Improved effectiveness by reducing defects for both existing and new equipment over their entire life spans. Defects include both product and process defects caused by the equipment, as well as the cycle defect caused by downtime.

- Significant involvement of operators in the maintenance of their equipment (autonomous maintenance).

- Effective preventative maintenance (PM).

- The use of small group activities to maintain and improve current equipment effectiveness and to set standards for new equipment maintainability.

- Improved safety.

TPM (and PM) will mitigate losses due to:

- Breakdowns (lost capacity).

- Setup and adjustment stoppages.

- Idling and minor stoppages.

- Reduced speed due to deterioration.

- Startup and yield stoppages (worn or broken tools).

- Defects and rework.

How do I do it?

1. **Implement** *autonomous maintenance.*

   • Autonomous maintenance assigns responsibility for day-to-day lubrication, cleaning, and adjustment of equipment to the operators of that equipment.

   • It is also suggested that operators assist when maintenance craftspeople work on their machines.

2. **Implement** *corrective maintenance.*

   • Corrective maintenance involves small cross-functional groups (including operators) actively evaluating the equipment and submitting improvement ideas aimed at preventing breakdowns and the conditions that cause them.

   • The aim is to make improvements that keep equipment from breaking down, facilitate inspection, repair, and use, and ensure safety. Having the results of daily inspections and the details of all breakdowns is crucial to the success of this step.

   • Frequently, a major cleaning of the equipment by the group is a logical start to both finding issues and establishing a team.

3. **Implement** *preventative maintenance.*

   • Preventative maintenance implies an interval-based service plan with the intervals based on data. In a TPM environment, much of the PM is done by the operators (autonomous maintenance).

   • Two common measurements are mean time between failures (MTBF) and mean time to repair (MTTR). TPM, or PM by itself, will not

©2002 GOAL/QPC,
Six Sigma Academy

function well if there is great variability in the MTBF.

4. **Implement** *maintenance prevention.*

   • The findings and knowledge gained as a result of work teams analyzing current machines should lead to any new equipment being specified to ensure it is reliable, maintainable, safe, and easy to use.

5. **Improve** *breakdown maintenance.*

   • Use TPM/PM activities to drive an improved response time for those cases when sudden machine failures occur.

Overall Equipment Effectiveness

Overall equipment effectiveness (OEE) is an index to measure the overall health of the equipment. It is used to identify the worst problems.

OEE = Availability x Performance x Quality

Where:

   • Availability = (Schedule time - Downtime)/ Schedule time
   • Performance = (Standard time x Output)/ Operating time
   • Quality = (Units total - Units defective)/ Units total

Ratio of planned vs. total maintenance

The ratio of planned maintenance vs. total maintenance is a useful metric to measure the status of TPM implementation.

Total maintenance is all recorded maintenance hours from all sources. Planned maintenance is the total maintenance less the maintenance done as a direct result of equipment breakdown. A monthly calculation of this ratio provides a barometer of the health of the TPM.

 **Control Plan**

Why use it?

A control plan provides an institutional memory of the status of a process and the measurements that define it. It provides for timely process troubleshooting and repair, and aids in training and audit activities. It becomes a living document within the process to sustain process improvements. It also documents the control activities of a Six Sigma project prior to completion.

What does it do?

A Six Sigma control plan is a set of documents that:

- Provides a point of reference among instructions, characteristics, and specifications.

- Links Critical to Satisfaction (CTS) characteristics to the operational details of the process.

- Encompasses several process areas including operating procedures, preventative maintenance, and gauge control (MSA). (**Note**: Because of space constraints, this chapter will be limited to discussion of operating procedures.)

- Provides prevention against process drift or deviation through identified measurement methods and responsibilities as well as decision rules and SOP references.

- Empowers local control of process corrective actions and resources.

- Can provide shutdown and/or quarantine activities.

- Links Key Process Input Variables (KPIVs) to Key Process Output Variables (KPOVs).

- Ensures that a Six Sigma project is ready for completion. If a control plan cannot be completed, at least one of the key elements (identification, specification, measurement, planned response to nonconformity, or control/responsibility) has not been defined or agreed to.

How do I do it?

A sample Control Plan is shown on the next page. The numbers in the figure correspond to the numbers in the description below.

The administrative section of the control plan (sections 1-3) provides key identification, approval, and document control information. The main body of the control plan (sections 4-8) provides substantive information on the process and reactions to out-of-control conditions. The last section (sections 9 and 10) links the control plan to the final FMEA.

1. The process information area should clearly and uniquely identify the process affected by the control plan.

2. The Black Belt (or Master Black Belt) and process owners should approve of the plan.

3. The document control section provides for identification, traceability, and retrieval of the control plan document itself. For a control plan to be effective, it must be a living document; therefore, the plan must contain space to document revisions.

4. The *Subprocess* and *Subprocess Step* fields identify and define the scope of the process being controlled.

5. The *CTS* fields indicate if the subprocess step generates a KPIV (directly linked to a KPOV) or a KPOV (directly affecting the customer).

A Six Sigma Control Plan

Process Name:	Prepared by:					Page: of
Customer:	Approved by:					Document #:
Location:	Approved by:					Revision Date:
Area:	Approved by:					Supercedes:

Subprocess	Subprocess Step	CTS		Specification Characteristic	Specification Requirement			Measurement Method	Sample Size	Frequency	Who Measures	Where Recorded	Decision Rule/ Corrective Action	SOP Reference
		KPIV	KPOV		LSL	Target	USL							
4		**5**		**6**	**7**			**8**					**9**	

1 **2** **3**

6. The *Specification Characteristic* field provides a succinct description of what is being checked/evaluated.

7. The *Specification Requirement* fields provide inspection criteria (specification limits or attribute screening criteria).

8. The *Measurement Method, Sample Size, Frequency, Who Measures,* and *Where Recorded* fields define the actual evaluation details.

9. The *Decision Rule/Corrective Action* and the *SOP Reference* fields provide response instructions if the process were to show nonconformance as a result of the inspection/evaluation activities as documented in the previous fields. It should include process shutdown or quarantine authority/procedures if appropriate, and show links to where other supporting documents, procedures, or policies (such as the organization's quality system) are documented.

10. An optional *Audit* column (not shown on this form) can provide clear linkage to ISO or QS audit systems. These audits can be on the output of the process (y's), on the inputs of the process (x's), or can be designed to ensure that the project controls are still in place.

©2002 GOAL/QPC,
Six Sigma Academy

A Sample Control Plan

Process Name: Panel Painting						Prepared by: Kelly Roff								Page: 1 of 1
Customer: ABC Construction (Ext)						Approved by: Page Right								Document #: PP-101-Rev C
Location: Building 1204-2						Approved by: Jordan Meyer								Revision Date: 19-Dec-02
Area: Post N4E8, Paint						Approved by:								Supersedes: Rev B

Subprocess	Subprocess Step	CTS KPIV	CTS KPOV	Characteristic Specification	Specification Requirement LSL	Specification Requirement Target	Specification Requirement USL	Measurement Method	Sample Size	Frequency	Who Measures	Where Recorded	Decision Rule/ Corrective Action	SOP Reference
Coat Application	Coating Application		X	Dosage	22		23	UIL-1700	1	1/hr	Techn	Process Log	Process shutdwn Chk feed mech. per SOP	PAC-121.2
	Coating Application	X		Coating thickness	17		18	UIL-1701	35 pts per panel	1/hr	Techn	Process Log	Process shutdwn/ Check nozzle per SOP	PAC-121.3

Appendix

Standard Z Table

Z	0	0.01	0.02	0.03	0.04	0.05	0.06	0.07	0.08	0.09
-4.0	0.00003	0.00003	0.00003	0.00003	0.00003	0.00003	0.00002	0.00002	0.00002	0.00002
-3.9	0.00005	0.00005	0.00004	0.00004	0.00004	0.00004	0.00004	0.00004	0.00003	0.00003
-3.8	0.00007	0.00007	0.00007	0.00006	0.00006	0.00006	0.00006	0.00005	0.00005	0.00005
-3.7	0.00011	0.00010	0.00010	0.00010	0.00009	0.00009	0.00008	0.00008	0.00008	0.00008
-3.6	0.00016	0.00015	0.00015	0.00014	0.00014	0.00013	0.00013	0.00012	0.00012	0.00011
-3.5	0.00023	0.00022	0.00022	0.00021	0.00020	0.00019	0.00019	0.00018	0.00017	0.00017
-3.4	0.00034	0.00032	0.00031	0.00030	0.00029	0.00028	0.00027	0.00026	0.00025	0.00024
-3.3	0.00048	0.00047	0.00045	0.00043	0.00042	0.00040	0.00039	0.00038	0.00036	0.00035
-3.2	0.00069	0.00066	0.00064	0.00062	0.00060	0.00058	0.00056	0.00054	0.00052	0.00050
-3.1	0.00097	0.00094	0.00090	0.00087	0.00084	0.00082	0.00079	0.00076	0.00074	0.00071
-3.0	0.00135	0.00131	0.00126	0.00122	0.00118	0.00114	0.00111	0.00107	0.00103	0.00100
-2.9	0.00187	0.00181	0.00175	0.00169	0.00164	0.00159	0.00154	0.00149	0.00144	0.00139
-2.8	0.00256	0.00248	0.00240	0.00233	0.00226	0.00219	0.00212	0.00205	0.00199	0.00193
-2.7	0.00347	0.00336	0.00326	0.00317	0.00307	0.00298	0.00289	0.00280	0.00272	0.00264
-2.6	0.00466	0.00453	0.00440	0.00427	0.00415	0.00402	0.00391	0.00379	0.00368	0.00357
-2.5	0.00621	0.00604	0.00587	0.00570	0.00554	0.00539	0.00523	0.00508	0.00494	0.00480
-2.4	0.00820	0.00798	0.00776	0.00755	0.00734	0.00714	0.00695	0.00676	0.00657	0.00639
-2.3	0.01072	0.01044	0.01017	0.00990	0.00964	0.00939	0.00914	0.00889	0.00866	0.00842
-2.2	0.01390	0.01355	0.01321	0.01287	0.01255	0.01222	0.01191	0.01160	0.01130	0.01101
-2.1	0.01786	0.01743	0.01700	0.01659	0.01618	0.01578	0.01539	0.01500	0.01463	0.01426
-2.0	0.02275	0.02222	0.02169	0.02118	0.02067	0.02018	0.01970	0.01923	0.01876	0.01831

Standard Z Table, continued

Z	0	0.01	0.02	0.03	0.04	0.05	0.06	0.07	0.08	0.09
-1.9	0.02872	0.02807	0.02743	0.02680	0.02619	0.02559	0.02500	0.02442	0.02385	0.02330
-1.8	0.03593	0.03515	0.03438	0.03362	0.03288	0.03216	0.03144	0.03074	0.03005	0.02938
-1.7	0.04456	0.04363	0.04272	0.04181	0.04093	0.04006	0.03920	0.03836	0.03754	0.03673
-1.6	0.05480	0.05370	0.05262	0.05155	0.05050	0.04947	0.04846	0.04746	0.04648	0.04551
-1.5	0.06681	0.06552	0.06425	0.06301	0.06178	0.06057	0.05938	0.05821	0.05705	0.05592
-1.4	0.08076	0.07927	0.07780	0.07636	0.07493	0.07353	0.07214	0.07078	0.06944	0.06811
-1.3	0.09680	0.09510	0.09342	0.09176	0.09012	0.08851	0.08691	0.08534	0.08379	0.08226
-1.2	0.11507	0.11314	0.11123	0.10935	0.10749	0.10565	0.10383	0.10204	0.10027	0.09852
-1.1	0.13566	0.13350	0.13136	0.12924	0.12714	0.12507	0.12302	0.12100	0.11900	0.11702
-1.0	0.15865	0.15625	0.15386	0.15150	0.14917	0.14686	0.14457	0.14231	0.14007	0.13786
-0.9	0.18406	0.18141	0.17878	0.17618	0.17361	0.17105	0.16853	0.16602	0.16354	0.16109
-0.8	0.21185	0.20897	0.20611	0.20327	0.20045	0.19766	0.19489	0.19215	0.18943	0.18673
-0.7	0.24196	0.23885	0.23576	0.23269	0.22965	0.22663	0.22363	0.22065	0.21769	0.21476
-0.6	0.27425	0.27093	0.26763	0.26434	0.26108	0.25784	0.25462	0.25143	0.24825	0.24509
-0.5	0.30853	0.30502	0.30153	0.29805	0.29460	0.29116	0.28774	0.28434	0.28095	0.27759
-0.4	0.34457	0.34090	0.33724	0.33359	0.32997	0.32635	0.32276	0.31917	0.31561	0.31206
-0.3	0.38209	0.37828	0.37448	0.37070	0.36692	0.36317	0.35942	0.35569	0.35197	0.34826
-0.2	0.42074	0.41683	0.41293	0.40904	0.40516	0.40129	0.39743	0.39358	0.38974	0.38590
-0.1	0.46017	0.45620	0.45224	0.44828	0.44433	0.44038	0.43644	0.43250	0.42857	0.42465
0.0	0.50000	0.49601	0.49202	0.48803	0.48404	0.48006	0.47607	0.47209	0.46811	0.46414

Z to DPMO
Conversion Table

Sigma Level* - Tenths	Sigma Level* - Hundredths									
	0.00	0.01	0.02	0.03	0.04	0.05	0.06	0.07	0.08	0.09
1.5	500,000	496,000	492,000	488,000	484,000	480,100	476,100	472,100	468,100	464,100
1.6	460,200	456,200	452,200	448,300	444,300	440,400	436,400	432,500	428,600	424,700
1.7	420,700	416,800	412,900	409,000	405,200	401,300	397,400	393,600	389,700	385,900
1.8	382,100	378,300	374,500	370,700	366,900	363,400	359,400	355,700	352,000	348,300
1.9	344,600	340,900	337,200	333,600	330,000	326,400	322,800	319,200	315,600	312,100
2.0	308,500	305,000	301,500	298,100	294,600	291,200	287,700	284,300	281,000	277,600
2.1	274,300	270,900	267,600	264,300	261,100	257,800	254,600	251,400	248,300	245,100
2.2	242,000	238,900	235,800	232,700	229,700	226,600	223,600	220,700	217,700	214,800
2.3	211,900	209,000	206,100	203,300	200,500	197,700	194,900	192,200	189,400	186,700
2.4	184,100	181,400	178,800	176,200	173,600	171,100	168,500	166,000	163,500	161,100
2.5	158,700	156,200	153,900	151,500	149,200	146,900	144,600	142,300	140,100	137,900
2.6	135,100	133,500	131,400	129,200	127,100	125,100	123,000	121,000	119,000	117,000
2.7	115,100	113,100	111,200	109,300	107,500	105,600	103,800	102,000	100,300	98,530
2.8	96,800	95,100	93,420	91,760	90,120	88,510	86,910	85,340	83,790	82,260
2.9	80,760	79,270	77,800	76,360	74,930	73,530	72,140	70,780	69,440	68,110
3.0	66,810	65,520	64,260	63,010	61,780	60,570	59,380	58,210	57,050	55,920
3.1	54,800	53,700	52,620	51,550	50,500	49,470	48,460	47,460	46,480	45,510
3.2	44,570	43,630	42,720	41,820	40,930	40,060	39,200	38,360	37,540	36,730
3.3	35,930	35,150	34,380	33,630	32,880	32,160	31,440	30,740	30,050	29,380
3.4	28,720	28,070	27,430	26,800	26,190	25,590	25,000	24,420	23,850	23,300
3.5	22,750	22,220	21,690	21,180	20,680	20,180	19,700	19,203	18,760	18,310
3.6	17,860	17,430	17,000	16,590	16,180	15,780	15,390	15,000	14,630	14,260
3.7	13,900	13,550	13,210	12,870	12,550	12,220	11,910	11,600	11,300	11,010
3.8	10,720	10,440	10,170	9,903	9,642	9,387	9,137	8,894	8,656	8,424
3.9	8,198	7,976	7,760	7,549	7,344	7,143	6,947	6,756	6,569	6,387
4.0	6,210	6,036	5,868	5,703	5,543	5,386	5,234	5,085	4,940	4,799

Z to DPMO
Conversion Table, continued

Sigma Level - Tenths	Sigma Level* - Hundredths									
	0.00	0.01	0.02	0.03	0.04	0.05	0.06	0.07	0.08	0.09
4.1	4,661	4,527	4,396	4,269	4,145	4,024	3,907	3,792	3,681	3,572
4.2	3,467	3,364	3,264	3,167	3,072	2,980	2,890	2,803	2,718	2,635
4.3	2,555	2,477	2,401	2,327	2,256	2,186	2,118	2,052	1,988	1,926
4.4	1,866	1,807	1,750	1,695	1,641	1,589	1,538	1,489	1,441	1,395
4.5	1,350	1,306	1,264	1,223	1,183	1,144	1,107	1,070	1,035	1,001
4.6	968	935	904	874	845	816	789	762	736	711
4.7	687	664	641	619	598	577	557	538	519	501
4.8	484	467	450	434	419	404	390	376	363	350
4.9	337	325	313	302	291	280	270	260	251	242
5.0	233	224	216	208	200	193	186	179	172	166
5.1	159	153	147	142	136	131	126	121	117	112
5.2	108	104	100	96	92	89	85	82	79	75
5.3	72	70	67	64	62	59	57	55	52	50
5.4	48	46	44	43	41	39	38	36	35	33
5.5	32	30	29	28	27	26	25	24	23	22
5.6	21.0	20.0	19.0	18.0	17.0	17.0	16.0	15.3	14.7	14.0
5.7	13.4	12.9	12.3	11.7	11.3	10.8	10.3	9.9	9.4	9.0
5.8	8.6	8.2	7.9	7.5	7.2	6.9	6.6	6.3	6.0	5.7
5.9	5.4	5.2	5.0	4.8	4.6	4.4	4.2	4.0	3.8	3.6
6.0	3.4	3.3	3.1	3.0	2.9	2.7	2.6	2.5	2.4	2.3

Example: 412,900 DPMO = 1.72 sigma, which, according to convention, is rounded-off to 1.7 sigma.
*1.5 sigma shift included.

Normal Distribution

z	0.00	0.01	0.02	0.03	0.04	0.05	0.06	0.07	0.08	0.09
0.0	0.5000	0.4960	0.4920	0.4880	0.4840	0.4801	0.4761	0.4721	0.4681	0.4641
0.1	0.4602	0.4562	0.4522	0.4483	0.4443	0.4404	0.4364	0.4325	0.4286	0.4247
0.2	0.4207	0.4168	0.4129	0.4090	0.4052	0.4013	0.3974	0.3936	0.3897	0.3859
0.3	0.3821	0.3783	0.3745	0.3707	0.3669	0.3632	0.3594	0.3557	0.3520	0.3483
0.4	0.3446	0.3409	0.3372	0.3336	0.3300	0.3264	0.3228	0.3192	0.3156	0.3121
0.5	0.3085	0.3050	0.3015	0.2981	0.2946	0.2912	0.2877	0.2843	0.2810	0.2776
0.6	0.2743	0.2709	0.2676	0.2643	0.2611	0.2578	0.2546	0.2514	0.2483	0.2451
0.7	0.2420	0.2389	0.2358	0.2327	0.2296	0.2266	0.2236	0.2206	0.2177	0.2148
0.8	0.2119	0.2090	0.2061	0.2033	0.2005	0.1977	0.1949	0.1922	0.1894	0.1867
0.9	0.1841	0.1814	0.1788	0.1762	0.1736	0.1711	0.1685	0.1660	0.1635	0.1611
1.0	0.1587	0.1562	0.1539	0.1515	0.1492	0.1469	0.1446	0.1423	0.1401	0.1379
1.1	0.1357	0.1335	0.1314	0.1292	0.1271	0.1251	0.1230	0.1210	0.1190	0.1170
1.2	0.1151	0.1131	0.1112	0.1093	0.1075	0.1056	0.1038	0.1020	0.1003	0.0985
1.3	0.0968	0.0951	0.0934	0.0918	0.0901	0.0885	0.0869	0.0853	0.0838	0.0823
1.4	0.0808	0.0793	0.0778	0.0764	0.0749	0.0735	0.0721	0.0708	0.0694	0.0681
1.5	0.0668	0.0655	0.0643	0.0630	0.0618	0.0606	0.0594	0.0582	0.0571	0.0559
1.6	0.0548	0.0537	0.0526	0.0516	0.0505	0.0495	0.0485	0.0475	0.0465	0.0455
1.7	0.0446	0.0436	0.0427	0.0418	0.0409	0.0401	0.0392	0.0384	0.0375	0.0367
1.8	0.0359	0.0351	0.0344	0.0336	0.0329	0.0322	0.0314	0.0307	0.0301	0.0294
1.9	0.0287	0.0281	0.0274	0.0268	0.0262	0.0256	0.0250	0.0244	0.0239	0.0233
2.0	0.0228	0.0222	0.0217	0.0212	0.0207	0.0202	0.0197	0.0192	0.0188	0.0183
2.1	0.0179	0.0174	0.0170	0.0166	0.0162	0.0158	0.0154	0.0150	0.0146	0.0143
2.2	0.0139	0.0136	0.0132	0.0129	0.0125	0.0122	0.0119	0.0116	0.0113	0.0110
2.3	0.0107	0.0104	0.0102	0.0099	0.0096	0.0094	0.0091	0.0089	0.0087	0.0084
2.4	0.0082	0.0080	0.0078	0.0075	0.0073	0.0071	0.0069	0.0068	0.0066	0.0064
2.5	0.0062	0.0060	0.0059	0.0057	0.0055	0.0054	0.0052	0.0051	0.0049	0.0048
2.6	0.0047	0.0045	0.0044	0.0043	0.0041	0.0040	0.0039	0.0038	0.0037	0.0036
2.7	0.0035	0.0034	0.0033	0.0032	0.0031	0.0030	0.0029	0.0028	0.0027	0.0026
2.8	0.0026	0.0025	0.0024	0.0023	0.0023	0.0022	0.0021	0.0021	0.0020	0.0019
2.9	0.0019	0.0018	0.0018	0.0017	0.0016	0.0016	0.0015	0.0015	0.0014	0.0014
3.0	0.0013	0.0013	0.0013	0.0012	0.0012	0.0011	0.0011	0.0011	0.0010	0.0010
3.1	0.0010	0.0009	0.0009	0.0009	0.0008	0.0008	0.0008	0.0008	0.0007	0.0007
3.2	0.0007	0.0007	0.0006	0.0006	0.0006	0.0006	0.0006	0.0005	0.0005	0.0005
3.3	0.0005	0.0005	0.0005	0.0004	0.0004	0.0004	0.0004	0.0004	0.0004	0.0003
3.4	0.0003	0.0003	0.0003	0.0003	0.0003	0.0003	0.0003	0.0003	0.0003	0.0002
3.5	0.0002	0.0002	0.0002	0.0002	0.0002	0.0002	0.0002	0.0002	0.0002	0.0002
3.6	0.0002	0.0002	0.0001	0.0001	0.0001	0.0001	0.0001	0.0001	0.0001	0.0001
3.7	0.0001	0.0001	0.0001	0.0001	0.0001	0.0001	0.0001	0.0001	0.0001	0.0001
3.8	0.0001	0.0001	0.0001	0.0001	0.0001	0.0001	0.0001	0.0001	0.0001	0.0001
3.9	0.0000	0.0000	0.0000	0.0000	0.0000	0.0000	0.0000	0.0000	0.0000	0.0000

Probability Points of t Distribution with ν Degrees of Freedom

ν	0.4	0.25	0.1	0.05	0.025	0.01	0.005	0.0025	0.001	0.0005
1	0.325	1.000	3.078	6.314	12.706	31.821	63.657	127.32	318.31	636.62
2	0.289	0.816	1.886	2.920	4.303	6.965	9.925	14.089	22.326	31.598
3	0.277	0.765	1.638	2.353	3.182	4.541	5.841	7.453	10.213	12.924
4	0.271	0.741	1.533	2.132	2.776	3.747	4.604	5.598	7.173	8.610
5	0.267	0.727	1.476	2.015	2.571	3.365	4.032	4.773	5.893	6.869
6	0.265	0.718	1.440	1.943	2.447	3.143	3.707	4.317	5.208	5.959
7	0.263	0.711	1.415	1.895	2.365	2.998	3.499	4.029	4.785	5.408
8	0.262	0.706	1.397	1.860	2.306	2.896	3.355	3.833	4.501	5.041
9	0.261	0.703	1.383	1.833	2.262	2.821	3.250	3.690	4.297	4.781
10	0.260	0.700	1.372	1.812	2.228	2.764	3.169	3.581	4.144	4.587
11	0.260	0.697	1.363	1.796	2.201	2.718	3.106	3.497	4.025	4.437
12	0.259	0.695	1.356	1.782	2.179	2.681	3.055	3.428	3.930	4.318
13	0.259	0.694	1.350	1.771	2.160	2.650	3.012	3.372	3.852	4.221
14	0.258	0.692	1.345	1.761	2.145	2.624	2.977	3.326	3.787	4.140
15	0.258	0.691	1.341	1.753	2.131	2.602	2.947	3.286	3.733	4.073
16	0.258	0.690	1.337	1.746	2.120	2.583	2.921	3.252	3.686	4.015
17	0.257	0.689	1.333	1.740	2.110	2.567	2.898	3.222	3.646	3.965
18	0.257	0.688	1.330	1.734	2.101	2.552	2.878	3.197	3.610	3.922
19	0.257	0.688	1.328	1.729	2.093	2.539	2.861	3.174	3.579	3.883
20	0.257	0.687	1.325	1.725	2.086	2.528	2.845	3.153	3.552	3.850
21	0.257	0.686	1.323	1.721	2.080	2.518	2.831	3.135	3.527	3.819
22	0.256	0.686	1.321	1.717	2.074	2.508	2.819	3.119	3.505	3.792
23	0.256	0.685	1.319	1.714	2.069	2.500	2.807	3.104	3.485	3.767
24	0.256	0.685	1.318	1.711	2.064	2.492	2.797	3.091	3.467	3.745
25	0.256	0.684	1.316	1.708	2.060	2.485	2.787	3.078	3.450	3.725
26	0.256	0.684	1.315	1.706	2.056	2.479	2.779	3.067	3.435	3.707
27	0.256	0.684	1.314	1.703	2.052	2.473	2.771	3.057	3.421	3.690
28	0.256	0.683	1.313	1.701	2.048	2.467	2.763	3.047	3.408	3.674
29	0.256	0.683	1.311	1.699	2.045	2.462	2.756	3.038	3.396	3.659
30	0.256	0.683	1.310	1.697	2.042	2.457	2.750	3.030	3.385	3.646
40	0.255	0.681	1.303	1.684	2.021	2.423	2.704	2.971	3.307	3.551
60	0.254	0.679	1.296	1.671	2.000	2.390	2.660	2.915	3.232	3.460
120	0.254	0.677	1.289	1.658	1.980	2.358	2.617	2.860	3.160	3.373
∞	0.253	0.674	1.282	1.645	1.960	2.326	2.576	2.807	3.090	3.291

Ordinates of t Distribution with v Degrees of Freedom

ordinate

v	0.00	0.25	0.50	0.75	1.00	1.25	1.50	1.75	2.00	2.25	2.50	2.75	3.00
1	0.318	0.300	0.255	0.204	0.159	0.124	0.098	0.078	0.064	0.053	0.044	0.037	0.032
2	0.354	0.338	0.296	0.244	0.193	0.149	0.114	0.088	0.068	0.053	0.042	0.034	0.027
3	0.368	0.353	0.313	0.261	0.207	0.159	0.120	0.090	0.068	0.051	0.039	0.030	0.023
4	0.375	0.361	0.322	0.270	0.215	0.164	0.123	0.091	0.066	0.049	0.036	0.026	0.020
5	0.380	0.366	0.328	0.276	0.220	0.168	0.125	0.091	0.065	0.047	0.033	0.024	0.017
6	0.383	0.369	0.332	0.280	0.223	0.170	0.126	0.090	0.064	0.045	0.032	0.022	0.016
7	0.385	0.372	0.335	0.283	0.226	0.172	0.126	0.090	0.063	0.044	0.030	0.021	0.014
8	0.387	0.373	0.337	0.285	0.228	0.173	0.127	0.090	0.062	0.043	0.029	0.019	0.013
9	0.388	0.375	0.338	0.287	0.229	0.174	0.127	0.090	0.062	0.042	0.028	0.018	0.012
10	0.389	0.376	0.340	0.288	0.230	0.175	0.127	0.090	0.061	0.041	0.027	0.018	0.011
11	0.390	0.377	0.341	0.289	0.231	0.176	0.128	0.089	0.061	0.040	0.026	0.017	0.011
12	0.391	0.378	0.342	0.290	0.232	0.176	0.128	0.089	0.060	0.040	0.026	0.016	0.010
13	0.391	0.378	0.343	0.291	0.233	0.177	0.128	0.089	0.060	0.039	0.025	0.016	0.010
14	0.392	0.379	0.343	0.292	0.234	0.177	0.128	0.089	0.060	0.039	0.025	0.015	0.010
15	0.392	0.380	0.344	0.292	0.234	0.177	0.128	0.089	0.059	0.038	0.024	0.015	0.009

Ordinates of t Distribution with v Degrees of Freedom, continued

ordinate

v	0.00	0.25	0.50	0.75	1.00	1.25	1.50	1.75	2.00	2.25	2.50	2.75	3.00
16	0.393	0.380	0.344	0.293	0.235	0.178	0.128	0.089	0.059	0.038	0.024	0.015	0.009
17	0.393	0.380	0.345	0.293	0.235	0.178	0.128	0.089	0.059	0.038	0.024	0.014	0.009
18	0.393	0.381	0.345	0.294	0.235	0.178	0.129	0.088	0.059	0.037	0.023	0.014	0.009
19	0.394	0.381	0.346	0.294	0.236	0.179	0.129	0.088	0.059	0.037	0.023	0.014	0.008
20	0.394	0.381	0.346	0.294	0.236	0.179	0.129	0.088	0.058	0.037	0.023	0.014	0.008
22	0.394	0.382	0.346	0.295	0.237	0.179	0.129	0.088	0.058	0.036	0.022	0.013	0.008
24	0.395	0.382	0.347	0.296	0.237	0.179	0.129	0.088	0.057	0.036	0.022	0.013	0.007
26	0.395	0.383	0.347	0.296	0.237	0.180	0.129	0.088	0.057	0.036	0.022	0.013	0.007
28	0.395	0.383	0.348	0.296	0.238	0.180	0.129	0.088	0.057	0.036	0.021	0.012	0.007
30	0.396	0.383	0.348	0.297	0.238	0.180	0.129	0.088	0.057	0.035	0.021	0.012	0.007
35	0.396	0.384	0.348	0.297	0.239	0.180	0.129	0.088	0.056	0.035	0.021	0.012	0.006
40	0.396	0.384	0.349	0.298	0.239	0.181	0.129	0.087	0.056	0.035	0.020	0.011	0.006
45	0.397	0.384	0.349	0.298	0.239	0.181	0.129	0.087	0.056	0.034	0.020	0.011	0.006
50	0.397	0.385	0.350	0.298	0.240	0.181	0.129	0.087	0.056	0.034	0.020	0.011	0.006
∞	0.399	0.387	0.352	0.301	0.242	0.183	0.130	0.086	0.054	0.032	0.018	0.009	0.004

χ^2 Distribution with v Degrees of Freedom

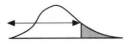

v	0.995	0.99	0.975	0.95	0.9	0.75	0.5	0.25	0.1	0.05	0.025	0.01	0.005	0.001
1	-	-	-	-	0.016	0.102	0.455	1.32	2.71	3.84	5.02	6.63	7.88	10.8
2	0.010	0.020	0.051	0.103	0.211	0.575	1.39	2.77	4.61	5.99	7.38	9.21	10.6	13.8
3	0.072	0.115	0.216	0.352	0.584	1.21	2.37	4.11	6.25	7.81	9.35	11.3	12.8	16.3
4	0.207	0.297	0.484	0.711	1.06	1.92	3.36	5.39	7.78	9.49	11.1	13.3	14.9	18.5
5	0.412	0.554	0.831	1.15	1.61	2.67	4.35	6.63	9.24	11.1	12.8	15.1	16.7	20.5
6	0.676	0.872	1.24	1.64	2.20	3.45	5.35	7.84	10.6	12.6	14.4	16.8	18.5	22.5
7	0.989	1.24	1.69	2.17	2.83	4.25	6.35	9.04	12.0	14.1	16.0	18.5	20.3	24.3
8	1.34	1.65	2.18	2.73	3.49	5.07	7.34	10.2	13.4	15.5	17.5	20.1	22.0	26.1
9	1.73	2.09	2.70	3.33	4.17	5.90	8.34	11.4	14.7	16.9	19.0	21.7	23.6	27.9
10	2.16	2.56	3.25	3.94	4.87	6.74	9.34	12.5	16.0	18.3	20.5	23.2	25.2	29.6
11	2.60	3.05	3.82	4.57	5.58	7.58	10.3	13.7	17.3	19.7	21.9	24.7	26.8	31.3
12	3.07	3.57	4.40	5.23	6.30	8.44	11.3	14.8	18.5	21.0	23.3	26.2	28.3	32.9
13	3.57	4.11	5.01	5.89	7.04	9.30	12.3	16.0	19.8	22.4	24.7	27.7	29.8	34.5
14	4.07	4.66	5.63	6.57	7.79	10.2	13.3	17.1	21.1	23.7	26.1	29.1	31.3	36.1
15	4.60	5.23	6.26	7.26	8.55	11.0	14.3	18.2	22.3	25.0	27.5	30.6	32.8	37.7

χ^2 Distribution with v Degrees of Freedom, continued

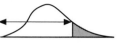

0.001	0.005	0.01	0.025	0.05	0.1	0.25	0.5	0.75	0.9	0.95	0.975	0.99	0.995	v
39.3	34.3	32.0	28.8	26.3	23.5	19.4	15.3	11.9	9.31	7.96	6.91	5.81	5.14	16
40.8	35.7	33.4	30.2	27.6	24.8	20.5	16.3	12.8	10.1	8.67	7.56	6.41	5.70	17
42.3	37.2	34.8	31.5	28.9	26.0	21.6	17.3	13.7	10.9	9.39	8.23	7.01	6.26	18
43.8	38.6	36.2	32.9	30.1	27.2	22.7	18.3	14.6	11.7	10.1	8.91	7.63	6.84	19
45.3	40.0	37.6	34.2	31.4	28.4	23.8	19.3	15.5	12.4	10.9	9.59	8.26	7.43	20
46.8	41.4	38.9	35.5	32.7	29.6	24.9	20.3	16.3	13.2	11.6	10.3	8.90	8.03	21
48.3	42.8	40.3	36.8	33.9	30.8	26.0	21.3	17.2	14.0	12.3	11.0	9.54	8.64	22
49.7	44.2	41.6	38.1	35.2	32.0	27.1	22.3	18.1	14.8	13.1	11.7	10.2	9.26	23
51.2	45.6	43.0	39.4	36.4	33.2	28.2	23.3	19.0	15.7	13.8	12.4	10.9	9.89	24
52.6	46.9	44.3	40.6	37.7	34.4	29.3	24.3	19.9	16.5	14.6	13.1	11.5	10.5	25
54.1	48.3	45.6	41.9	38.9	35.6	30.4	25.3	20.8	17.3	15.4	13.8	12.2	11.2	26
55.5	49.6	47.0	43.2	40.1	36.7	31.5	26.3	21.7	18.1	16.2	14.6	12.9	11.8	27
56.9	51.0	48.3	44.5	41.3	37.9	32.6	27.3	22.7	18.9	16.9	15.3	13.6	12.5	28
58.3	52.3	49.6	45.7	42.6	39.1	33.7	28.3	23.6	19.8	17.7	16.0	14.3	13.1	29
59.7	53.7	50.9	47.0	43.8	40.3	34.8	29.3	24.5	20.6	18.5	16.8	15.0	13.8	30

F Distribution: Upper 25% Points

v_2\\v_1	1	2	3	4	5	6	7	8	9
1	5.83	7.50	8.20	8.58	8.82	8.98	9.10	9.19	9.26
2	2.57	3.00	3.15	3.23	3.28	3.31	3.34	3.35	3.37
3	2.02	2.28	2.36	2.39	2.41	2.42	2.43	2.44	2.44
4	1.81	2.00	2.05	2.06	2.07	2.08	2.08	2.08	2.08
5	1.69	1.85	1.88	1.89	1.89	1.89	1.89	1.89	1.89
6	1.62	1.76	1.78	1.79	1.79	1.78	1.78	1.78	1.77
7	1.57	1.70	1.72	1.72	1.71	1.71	1.70	1.70	1.69
8	1.54	1.66	1.67	1.66	1.66	1.65	1.64	1.64	1.63
9	1.51	1.62	1.63	1.63	1.62	1.61	1.60	1.60	1.59
10	1.49	1.60	1.60	1.59	1.59	1.58	1.57	1.56	1.56
11	1.47	1.58	1.58	1.57	1.56	1.55	1.54	1.53	1.53
12	1.46	1.56	1.56	1.55	1.54	1.53	1.52	1.51	1.51
13	1.45	1.55	1.55	1.53	1.52	1.51	1.50	1.49	1.49
14	1.44	1.53	1.53	1.52	1.51	1.50	1.49	1.48	1.47
15	1.43	1.52	1.52	1.51	1.49	1.48	1.47	1.46	1.46
16	1.42	1.51	1.51	1.50	1.48	1.47	1.46	1.45	1.44
17	1.42	1.51	1.50	1.49	1.47	1.46	1.45	1.44	1.43
18	1.41	1.50	1.49	1.48	1.46	1.45	1.44	1.43	1.42
19	1.41	1.49	1.49	1.47	1.46	1.44	1.43	1.42	1.41
20	1.40	1.49	1.48	1.47	1.45	1.44	1.43	1.42	1.41
21	1.40	1.48	1.48	1.46	1.44	1.43	1.42	1.41	1.40
22	1.40	1.48	1.47	1.45	1.44	1.42	1.41	1.40	1.39
23	1.39	1.47	1.47	1.45	1.43	1.42	1.41	1.40	1.39
24	1.39	1.47	1.46	1.44	1.43	1.41	1.40	1.39	1.38
25	1.39	1.47	1.46	1.44	1.42	1.41	1.40	1.39	1.38
26	1.38	1.46	1.45	1.44	1.42	1.41	1.39	1.38	1.37
27	1.38	1.46	1.45	1.43	1.42	1.40	1.39	1.38	1.37
28	1.38	1.46	1.45	1.43	1.41	1.40	1.39	1.38	1.37
29	1.38	1.45	1.45	1.43	1.41	1.40	1.38	1.37	1.36
30	1.38	1.45	1.44	1.42	1.41	1.39	1.38	1.37	1.36
40	1.36	1.44	1.42	1.40	1.39	1.37	1.36	1.35	1.34
60	1.35	1.42	1.41	1.38	1.37	1.35	1.33	1.32	1.31
120	1.34	1.40	1.39	1.37	1.35	1.33	1.31	1.30	1.29
∞	1.32	1.39	1.37	1.35	1.33	1.31	1.29	1.28	1.27

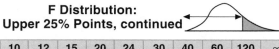

F Distribution:
Upper 25% Points, continued

v_2\\v_1	10	12	15	20	24	30	40	60	120	∞
1	9.32	9.41	9.49	9.58	9.63	9.67	9.71	9.76	9.80	9.85
2	3.38	3.39	3.41	3.43	3.43	3.44	3.45	3.46	3.47	3.48
3	2.44	2.45	2.46	2.46	2.46	2.47	2.47	2.47	2.47	2.47
4	2.08	2.08	2.08	2.08	2.08	2.08	2.08	2.08	2.08	2.08
5	1.89	1.89	1.89	1.88	1.88	1.88	1.88	1.87	1.87	1.87
6	1.77	1.77	1.76	1.76	1.75	1.75	1.75	1.74	1.74	1.74
7	1.69	1.68	1.68	1.67	1.67	1.66	1.66	1.65	1.65	1.65
8	1.63	1.62	1.62	1.61	1.60	1.60	1.59	1.59	1.58	1.58
9	1.59	1.58	1.57	1.56	1.56	1.55	1.54	1.54	1.53	1.53
10	1.55	1.54	1.53	1.52	1.52	1.51	1.51	1.50	1.49	1.48
11	1.52	1.51	1.50	1.49	1.49	1.48	1.47	1.47	1.46	1.45
12	1.50	1.49	1.48	1.47	1.46	1.45	1.45	1.44	1.43	1.42
13	1.48	1.47	1.46	1.45	1.44	1.43	1.42	1.42	1.41	1.40
14	1.46	1.45	1.44	1.43	1.42	1.41	1.41	1.40	1.39	1.38
15	1.45	1.44	1.43	1.41	1.41	1.40	1.39	1.38	1.37	1.36
16	1.44	1.43	1.41	1.40	1.39	1.38	1.37	1.36	1.35	1.34
17	1.43	1.41	1.40	1.39	1.38	1.37	1.36	1.35	1.34	1.33
18	1.42	1.40	1.39	1.38	1.37	1.36	1.35	1.34	1.33	1.32
19	1.41	1.40	1.38	1.37	1.36	1.35	1.34	1.33	1.32	1.30
20	1.40	1.39	1.37	1.36	1.35	1.34	1.33	1.32	1.31	1.29
21	1.39	1.38	1.37	1.35	1.34	1.33	1.32	1.31	1.30	1.28
22	1.39	1.37	1.36	1.34	1.33	1.32	1.31	1.30	1.29	1.28
23	1.38	1.37	1.35	1.34	1.33	1.32	1.31	1.30	1.28	1.27
24	1.38	1.36	1.35	1.33	1.32	1.31	1.30	1.29	1.28	1.26
25	1.37	1.36	1.34	1.33	1.32	1.31	1.29	1.28	1.27	1.25
26	1.37	1.35	1.34	1.32	1.31	1.30	1.29	1.28	1.26	1.25
27	1.36	1.35	1.33	1.32	1.31	1.30	1.28	1.27	1.26	1.24
28	1.36	1.34	1.33	1.31	1.30	1.29	1.28	1.27	1.25	1.24
29	1.35	1.34	1.32	1.31	1.30	1.29	1.27	1.26	1.25	1.23
30	1.35	1.34	1.32	1.30	1.29	1.28	1.27	1.26	1.24	1.23
40	1.33	1.31	1.30	1.28	1.26	1.25	1.24	1.22	1.21	1.19
60	1.30	1.29	1.27	1.25	1.24	1.22	1.21	1.19	1.17	1.15
120	1.28	1.26	1.24	1.22	1.21	1.19	1.18	1.16	1.13	1.10
∞	1.25	1.24	1.22	1.19	1.18	1.16	1.14	1.12	1.08	1.00

F Distribution: Upper 10% Points

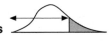

v_2 \ v_1	1	2	3	4	5	6	7	8	9
1	39.86	49.50	53.59	55.83	57.24	58.20	58.91	59.44	59.86
2	8.53	9.00	9.16	9.24	9.29	9.33	9.35	9.37	9.38
3	5.54	5.46	5.39	5.34	5.31	5.28	5.27	5.25	5.24
4	4.54	4.32	4.19	4.11	4.05	4.01	3.98	3.95	3.94
5	4.06	3.78	3.62	3.52	3.45	3.40	3.37	3.34	3.32
6	3.78	3.46	3.29	3.18	3.11	3.05	3.01	2.98	2.96
7	3.59	3.26	3.07	2.96	2.88	2.83	2.78	2.75	2.72
8	3.46	3.11	2.92	2.81	2.73	2.67	2.62	2.59	2.56
9	3.36	3.01	2.81	2.69	2.61	2.55	2.51	2.47	2.44
10	3.29	2.92	2.73	2.61	2.52	2.46	2.41	2.38	2.35
11	3.23	2.86	2.66	2.54	2.45	2.39	2.34	2.30	2.27
12	3.18	2.81	2.61	2.48	2.39	2.33	2.28	2.24	2.21
13	3.14	2.76	2.56	2.43	2.35	2.28	2.23	2.20	2.16
14	3.10	2.73	2.52	2.39	2.31	2.24	2.19	2.15	2.12
15	3.07	2.70	2.49	2.36	2.27	2.21	2.16	2.12	2.09
16	3.05	2.67	2.46	2.33	2.24	2.18	2.13	2.09	2.06
17	3.03	2.64	2.44	2.31	2.22	2.15	2.10	2.06	2.03
18	3.01	2.62	2.42	2.29	2.20	2.13	2.08	2.04	2.00
19	2.99	2.61	2.40	2.27	2.18	2.11	2.06	2.02	1.98
20	2.97	2.59	2.38	2.25	2.16	2.09	2.04	2.00	1.96
21	2.96	2.57	2.36	2.23	2.14	2.08	2.02	1.98	1.95
22	2.95	2.56	2.35	2.22	2.13	2.06	2.01	1.97	1.93
23	2.94	2.55	2.34	2.21	2.11	2.05	1.99	1.95	1.92
24	2.93	2.54	2.33	2.19	2.10	2.04	1.98	1.94	1.91
25	2.92	2.53	2.32	2.18	2.09	2.02	1.97	1.93	1.89
26	2.91	2.52	2.31	2.17	2.08	2.01	1.96	1.92	1.88
27	2.90	2.51	2.30	2.17	2.07	2.00	1.95	1.91	1.87
28	2.89	2.50	2.29	2.16	2.06	2.00	1.94	1.90	1.87
29	2.89	2.50	2.28	2.15	2.06	1.99	1.93	1.89	1.86
30	2.88	2.49	2.28	2.14	2.05	1.98	1.93	1.88	1.85
40	2.84	2.44	2.23	2.09	2.00	1.93	1.87	1.83	1.79
60	2.79	2.39	2.18	2.04	1.95	1.87	1.82	1.77	1.74
120	2.75	2.35	2.13	1.99	1.90	1.82	1.77	1.72	1.68
∞	2.71	2.30	2.08	1.94	1.85	1.77	1.72	1.67	1.63

F Distribution:
Upper 10% Points, continued

v_1 / v_2	10	12	15	20	24	30	40	60	120	∞
1	60.19	60.71	61.22	61.74	62.00	62.26	62.53	62.79	63.06	63.33
2	9.39	9.41	9.42	9.44	9.45	9.46	9.47	9.47	9.48	9.49
3	5.23	5.22	5.20	5.18	5.18	5.17	5.16	5.15	5.14	5.13
4	3.92	3.90	3.87	3.84	3.83	3.82	3.80	3.79	3.78	3.76
5	3.30	3.27	3.24	3.21	3.19	3.17	3.16	3.14	3.12	3.10
6	2.94	2.90	2.87	2.84	2.82	2.80	2.78	2.76	2.74	2.72
7	2.70	2.67	2.63	2.59	2.58	2.56	2.54	2.51	2.49	2.47
8	2.54	2.50	2.46	2.42	2.40	2.38	2.36	2.34	2.32	2.29
9	2.42	2.38	2.34	2.30	2.28	2.25	2.23	2.21	2.18	2.16
10	2.32	2.28	2.24	2.20	2.18	2.16	2.13	2.11	2.08	2.06
11	2.25	2.21	2.17	2.12	2.10	2.08	2.05	2.03	2.00	1.97
12	2.19	2.15	2.10	2.06	2.04	2.01	1.99	1.96	1.93	1.90
13	2.14	2.10	2.05	2.01	1.98	1.96	1.93	1.90	1.88	1.85
14	2.10	2.05	2.01	1.96	1.94	1.91	1.89	1.86	1.83	1.80
15	2.06	2.02	1.97	1.92	1.90	1.87	1.85	1.82	1.79	1.76
16	2.03	1.99	1.94	1.89	1.87	1.84	1.81	1.78	1.75	1.72
17	2.00	1.96	1.91	1.86	1.84	1.81	1.78	1.75	1.72	1.69
18	1.98	1.93	1.89	1.84	1.81	1.78	1.75	1.72	1.69	1.66
19	1.96	1.91	1.86	1.81	1.79	1.76	1.73	1.70	1.67	1.63
20	1.94	1.89	1.84	1.79	1.77	1.74	1.71	1.68	1.64	1.61
21	1.92	1.87	1.83	1.78	1.75	1.72	1.69	1.66	1.62	1.59
22	1.90	1.86	1.81	1.76	1.73	1.70	1.67	1.64	1.60	1.57
23	1.89	1.84	1.80	1.74	1.72	1.69	1.66	1.62	1.59	1.55
24	1.88	1.83	1.78	1.73	1.70	1.67	1.64	1.61	1.57	1.53
25	1.87	1.82	1.77	1.72	1.69	1.66	1.63	1.59	1.56	1.52
26	1.86	1.81	1.76	1.71	1.68	1.65	1.61	1.58	1.54	1.50
27	1.85	1.80	1.75	1.70	1.67	1.64	1.60	1.57	1.53	1.49
28	1.84	1.79	1.74	1.69	1.66	1.63	1.59	1.56	1.52	1.48
29	1.83	1.78	1.73	1.68	1.65	1.62	1.58	1.55	1.51	1.47
30	1.82	1.77	1.72	1.67	1.64	1.61	1.57	1.54	1.50	1.46
40	1.76	1.71	1.66	1.61	1.57	1.54	1.51	1.47	1.42	1.38
60	1.71	1.66	1.60	1.54	1.51	1.48	1.44	1.40	1.35	1.29
120	1.65	1.60	1.55	1.48	1.45	1.41	1.37	1.32	1.26	1.19
∞	1.60	1.55	1.49	1.42	1.38	1.34	1.30	1.24	1.17	1.00

F Distribution:
Upper 5% Points

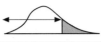

v_2 \ v_1	1	2	3	4	5	6	7	8	9
1	161.4	199.5	215.7	224.6	230.2	234.0	236.8	238.9	240.5
2	18.51	19.00	19.16	19.25	19.30	19.33	19.35	19.37	19.38
3	10.13	9.55	9.28	9.12	9.01	8.94	8.89	8.85	8.81
4	7.71	6.94	6.59	6.39	6.26	6.16	6.09	6.04	6.00
5	6.61	5.79	5.41	5.19	5.05	4.95	4.88	4.82	4.77
6	5.99	5.14	4.76	4.53	4.39	4.28	4.21	4.15	4.10
7	5.59	4.74	4.35	4.12	3.97	3.87	3.79	3.73	3.68
8	5.32	4.46	4.07	3.84	3.69	3.58	3.50	3.44	3.39
9	5.12	4.26	3.86	3.63	3.48	3.37	3.29	3.23	3.18
10	4.96	4.10	3.71	3.48	3.33	3.22	3.14	3.07	3.02
11	4.84	3.98	3.59	3.36	3.20	3.09	3.01	2.95	2.90
12	4.75	3.89	3.49	3.26	3.11	3.00	2.91	2.85	2.80
13	4.67	3.81	3.41	3.18	3.03	2.92	2.83	2.77	2.71
14	4.60	3.74	3.34	3.11	2.96	2.85	2.76	2.70	2.65
15	4.54	3.68	3.29	3.06	2.90	2.79	2.71	2.64	2.59
16	4.49	3.63	3.24	3.01	2.85	2.74	2.66	2.59	2.54
17	4.45	3.59	3.20	2.96	2.81	2.70	2.61	2.55	2.49
18	4.41	3.55	3.16	2.93	2.77	2.66	2.58	2.51	2.46
19	4.38	3.52	3.13	2.90	2.74	2.63	2.54	2.48	2.42
20	4.35	3.49	3.10	2.87	2.71	2.60	2.51	2.45	2.39
21	4.32	3.47	3.07	2.84	2.68	2.57	2.49	2.42	2.37
22	4.30	3.44	3.05	2.82	2.66	2.55	2.46	2.40	2.34
23	4.28	3.42	3.03	2.80	2.64	2.53	2.44	2.37	2.32
24	4.26	3.40	3.01	2.78	2.62	2.51	2.42	2.36	2.30
25	4.24	3.39	2.99	2.76	2.60	2.49	2.40	2.34	2.28
26	4.23	3.37	2.98	2.74	2.59	2.47	2.39	2.32	2.27
27	4.21	3.35	2.96	2.73	2.57	2.46	2.37	2.31	2.25
28	4.20	3.34	2.95	2.71	2.56	2.45	2.36	2.29	2.24
29	4.18	3.33	2.93	2.70	2.55	2.43	2.35	2.28	2.22
30	4.17	3.32	2.92	2.69	2.53	2.42	2.33	2.27	2.21
40	4.08	3.23	2.84	2.61	2.45	2.34	2.25	2.18	2.12
60	4.00	3.15	2.76	2.53	2.37	2.25	2.17	2.10	2.04
120	3.92	3.07	2.68	2.45	2.29	2.17	2.09	2.02	1.96
∞	3.84	3.00	2.60	2.37	2.21	2.10	2.01	1.94	1.88

F Distribution:
Upper 5% Points, continued

v_2 \ v_1	10	12	15	20	24	30	40	60	120	∞
1	241.9	243.9	245.9	248.0	249.1	250.1	251.1	252.2	253.3	254.3
2	19.40	19.41	19.43	19.45	19.45	19.46	19.47	19.48	19.49	19.50
3	8.79	8.74	8.70	8.66	8.64	8.62	8.59	8.57	8.55	8.53
4	5.96	5.91	5.86	5.80	5.77	5.75	5.72	5.69	5.66	5.63
5	4.74	4.68	4.62	4.56	4.53	4.50	4.46	4.43	4.40	4.36
6	4.06	4.00	3.94	3.87	3.84	3.81	3.77	3.74	3.70	3.67
7	3.64	3.57	3.51	3.44	3.41	3.38	3.34	3.30	3.27	3.23
8	3.35	3.28	3.22	3.15	3.12	3.08	3.04	3.01	2.97	2.93
9	3.14	3.07	3.01	2.94	2.90	2.86	2.83	2.79	2.75	2.71
10	2.98	2.91	2.85	2.77	2.74	2.70	2.66	2.62	2.58	2.54
11	2.85	2.79	2.72	2.65	2.61	2.57	2.53	2.49	2.45	2.40
12	2.75	2.69	2.62	2.54	2.51	2.47	2.43	2.38	2.34	2.30
13	2.67	2.60	2.53	2.46	2.42	2.38	2.34	2.30	2.25	2.21
14	2.60	2.53	2.46	2.39	2.35	2.31	2.27	2.22	2.18	2.13
15	2.54	2.48	2.40	2.33	2.29	2.25	2.20	2.16	2.11	2.07
16	2.49	2.42	2.35	2.28	2.24	2.19	2.15	2.11	2.06	2.01
17	2.45	2.38	2.31	2.23	2.19	2.15	2.10	2.06	2.01	1.96
18	2.41	2.34	2.27	2.19	2.15	2.11	2.06	2.02	1.97	1.92
19	2.38	2.31	2.23	2.16	2.11	2.07	2.03	1.98	1.93	1.88
20	2.35	2.28	2.20	2.12	2.08	2.04	1.99	1.95	1.90	1.84
21	2.32	2.25	2.18	2.10	2.05	2.01	1.96	1.92	1.87	1.81
22	2.30	2.23	2.15	2.07	2.03	1.98	1.94	1.89	1.84	1.78
23	2.27	2.20	2.13	2.05	2.01	1.96	1.91	1.86	1.81	1.76
24	2.25	2.18	2.11	2.03	1.98	1.94	1.89	1.84	1.79	1.73
25	2.24	2.16	2.09	2.01	1.96	1.92	1.87	1.82	1.77	1.71
26	2.22	2.15	2.07	1.99	1.95	1.90	1.85	1.80	1.75	1.69
27	2.20	2.13	2.06	1.97	1.93	1.88	1.84	1.79	1.73	1.67
28	2.19	2.12	2.04	1.96	1.91	1.87	1.82	1.77	1.71	1.65
29	2.18	2.10	2.03	1.94	1.90	1.85	1.81	1.75	1.70	1.64
30	2.16	2.09	2.01	1.93	1.89	1.84	1.79	1.74	1.68	1.62
40	2.08	2.00	1.92	1.84	1.79	1.74	1.69	1.64	1.58	1.51
60	1.99	1.92	1.84	1.75	1.70	1.65	1.59	1.53	1.47	1.39
120	1.91	1.83	1.75	1.66	1.61	1.55	1.50	1.43	1.35	1.25
∞	1.83	1.75	1.67	1.57	1.52	1.46	1.39	1.32	1.22	1.00

F Distribution: Upper 1% Points

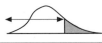

v_2 \ v_1	1	2	3	4	5	6	7	8	9
1	4052	4999.50	5403	5625	5764	5859	5928	5982	6022
2	98.50	99.00	99.17	99.25	99.30	99.33	99.36	99.37	99.39
3	34.12	30.82	29.46	28.71	28.24	27.91	27.67	27.49	27.35
4	21.20	18.00	16.69	15.98	15.52	15.21	14.98	14.80	14.66
5	16.26	13.27	12.06	11.39	10.97	10.67	10.46	10.29	10.16
6	13.75	10.92	9.78	9.15	8.75	8.47	8.26	8.10	7.98
7	12.25	9.55	8.45	7.85	7.46	7.19	6.99	6.84	6.72
8	11.26	8.65	7.59	7.01	6.63	6.37	6.18	6.03	5.91
9	10.56	8.02	6.99	6.42	6.06	5.80	5.61	5.47	5.35
10	10.04	7.56	6.55	5.99	5.64	5.39	5.20	5.06	4.94
11	9.65	7.21	6.22	5.67	5.32	5.07	4.89	4.74	4.63
12	9.33	6.93	5.95	5.41	5.06	4.82	4.64	4.50	4.39
13	9.07	6.70	5.74	5.21	4.86	4.62	4.44	4.30	4.19
14	8.86	6.51	5.56	5.04	4.69	4.46	4.28	4.14	4.03
15	8.68	6.36	5.42	4.89	4.56	4.32	4.14	4.00	3.89
16	8.53	6.23	5.29	4.77	4.44	4.20	4.03	3.89	3.78
17	8.40	6.11	5.18	4.67	4.34	4.10	3.93	3.79	3.68
18	8.29	6.01	5.09	4.58	4.25	4.01	3.84	3.71	3.60
19	8.18	5.93	5.01	4.50	4.17	3.94	3.77	3.63	3.52
20	8.10	5.85	4.94	4.43	4.10	3.87	3.70	3.56	3.46
21	8.02	5.78	4.87	4.37	4.04	3.81	3.64	3.51	3.40
22	7.95	5.72	4.82	4.31	3.99	3.76	3.59	3.45	3.35
23	7.88	5.66	4.76	4.26	3.94	3.71	3.54	3.41	3.30
24	7.82	5.61	4.72	4.22	3.90	3.67	3.50	3.36	3.26
25	7.77	5.57	4.68	4.18	3.85	3.63	3.46	3.32	3.22
26	7.72	5.53	4.64	4.14	3.82	3.59	3.42	3.29	3.18
27	7.68	5.49	4.60	4.11	3.78	3.56	3.39	3.26	3.15
28	7.64	5.45	4.57	4.07	3.75	3.53	3.36	3.23	3.12
29	7.60	5.42	4.54	4.04	3.73	3.50	3.33	3.20	3.09
30	7.56	5.39	4.51	4.02	3.70	3.47	3.30	3.17	3.07
40	7.31	5.18	4.31	3.83	3.51	3.29	3.12	2.99	2.89
60	7.08	4.98	4.13	3.65	3.34	3.12	2.95	2.82	2.72
120	6.85	4.79	3.95	3.48	3.17	2.96	2.79	2.66	2.56
∞	6.63	4.61	3.78	3.32	3.02	2.80	2.64	2.51	2.41

F Distribution:
Upper 1% Points, continued

v₂＼v₁	10	12	15	20	24	30	40	60	120	∞
1	6056	6106	6157	6209	6235	6261	6287	6313	6339	6366
2	99.40	99.42	99.43	99.45	99.46	99.47	99.47	99.48	99.49	99.50
3	27.23	27.05	26.87	26.69	26.60	26.50	26.41	26.32	26.22	26.13
4	14.55	14.37	14.20	14.02	13.93	13.84	13.75	13.65	13.56	13.46
5	10.05	9.89	9.72	9.55	9.47	9.38	9.29	9.20	9.11	9.02
6	7.87	7.72	7.56	7.40	7.31	7.23	7.14	7.06	6.97	6.88
7	6.62	6.47	6.31	6.16	6.07	5.99	5.91	5.82	5.74	5.65
8	5.81	5.67	5.52	5.36	5.28	5.20	5.12	5.03	4.95	4.86
9	5.26	5.11	4.96	4.81	4.73	4.65	4.57	4.48	4.40	4.31
10	4.85	4.71	4.56	4.41	4.33	4.25	4.17	4.08	4.00	3.91
11	4.54	4.40	4.25	4.10	4.02	3.94	3.86	3.78	3.69	3.60
12	4.30	4.16	4.01	3.86	3.78	3.70	3.62	3.54	3.45	3.36
13	4.10	3.96	3.82	3.66	3.59	3.51	3.43	3.34	3.25	3.17
14	3.94	3.80	3.66	3.51	3.43	3.35	3.27	3.18	3.09	3.00
15	3.80	3.67	3.52	3.37	3.29	3.21	3.13	3.05	2.96	2.87
16	3.69	3.55	3.41	3.26	3.18	3.10	3.02	2.93	2.84	2.75
17	3.59	3.46	3.31	3.16	3.08	3.00	2.92	2.83	2.75	2.65
18	3.51	3.37	3.23	3.08	3.00	2.92	2.84	2.75	2.66	2.57
19	3.43	3.30	3.15	3.00	2.92	2.84	2.76	2.67	2.58	2.49
20	3.37	3.23	3.09	2.94	2.86	2.78	2.69	2.61	2.52	2.42
21	3.31	3.17	3.03	2.88	2.80	2.72	2.64	2.55	2.46	2.36
22	3.26	3.12	2.98	2.83	2.75	2.67	2.58	2.50	2.40	2.31
23	3.21	3.07	2.93	2.78	2.70	2.62	2.54	2.45	2.35	2.26
24	3.17	3.03	2.89	2.74	2.66	2.58	2.49	2.40	2.31	2.21
25	3.13	2.99	2.85	2.70	2.62	2.54	2.45	2.36	2.27	2.17
26	3.09	2.96	2.81	2.66	2.58	2.50	2.42	2.33	2.23	2.13
27	3.06	2.93	2.78	2.63	2.55	2.47	2.38	2.29	2.20	2.10
28	3.03	2.90	2.75	2.60	2.52	2.44	2.35	2.26	2.17	2.06
29	3.00	2.87	2.73	2.57	2.49	2.41	2.33	2.23	2.14	2.03
30	2.98	2.84	2.70	2.55	2.47	2.39	2.30	2.21	2.11	2.01
40	2.80	2.66	2.52	2.37	2.29	2.20	2.11	2.02	1.92	1.80
60	2.63	2.50	2.35	2.20	2.12	2.03	1.94	1.84	1.73	1.60
120	2.47	2.34	2.19	2.03	1.95	1.86	1.76	1.66	1.53	1.38
∞	2.32	2.18	2.04	1.88	1.79	1.70	1.59	1.47	1.32	1.00

Sigma Conversion Chart

Long-term Yield	Long-term Sigma	Short-term Sigma	Defects per Million
99.99966%	4.5	6.0	3.4
99.9995%	4.4	5.9	5
99.9992%	4.3	5.8	8
99.9990%	4.2	5.7	10
99.9980%	4.1	5.6	20
99.9970%	4.0	5.5	30
99.9960%	3.9	5.4	40
99.9930%	3.8	5.3	70
99.9900%	3.7	5.2	100
99.9850%	3.6	5.1	150
99.9770%	3.5	5.0	230
99.9670%	3.4	4.9	330
99.9520%	3.3	4.8	480
99.9320%	3.2	4.7	680
99.9040%	3.1	4.6	960
99.8650%	3.0	4.5	1,350
99.8140%	2.9	4.4	1,860
99.7450%	2.8	4.3	2,550
99.6540%	2.7	4.2	3,460
99.5340%	2.6	4.1	4,660
99.3790%	2.5	4.0	6,210
99.1810%	2.4	3.9	8,190
98.930%	2.3	3.8	10,700
98.610%	2.2	3.7	13,900
98.220%	2.1	3.6	17,800
97.730%	2.0	3.5	22,700
97.130%	1.9	3.4	28,700

Long-term Yield	Long-term Sigma	Short-term Sigma	Defects per Million
96.410%	1.8	3.3	35,900
95.540%	1.7	3.2	44,600
94.520%	1.6	3.1	54,800
93.320%	1.5	3.0	66,800
91.920%	1.4	2.9	80,800
90.320%	1.3	2.8	96,800
88.50%	1.2	2.7	115,000
86.50%	1.1	2.6	135,000
84.20%	1.0	2.5	158,000
81.60%	0.9	2.4	184,000
78.80%	0.8	2.3	212,000
75.80%	0.7	2.2	242,000
72.60%	0.6	2.1	274,000
69.20%	0.5	2.0	308,000
65.60%	0.4	1.9	344,000
61.80%	0.3	1.8	382,000
58.00%	0.2	1.7	420,000
54.00%	0.1	1.6	460,000
50.00%	0.0	1.5	500,000
46.00%	-0.1	1.4	540,000
42.00%	-0.2	1.3	580,000
38.00%	-0.3	1.2	620,000
34.00%	-0.4	1.1	660,000
31.00%	-0.5	1.0	690,000
27.00%	-0.6	0.9	730,000
24.00%	-0.7	0.8	760,000

Note: The 1.5 sigma shift is included in this chart.

Index